Stranger West

John E Olsen

ISBN: ISBN: 9781099515606

DEDICATION

This book is dedicated to my wife, Annie. Without you, these stories, like me, would be sitting dusty on the shelf. Thanks for giving me a new life, a fresh start, and the ability to believe in myself.

Contents

Acknowledgments

I would like to thank my reader and those who have allowed me to write their stories, you are all fantastic people. Remember, you are not alone.

Intro

My journey into the unknown started when I was very young. I grew up in a home that was over 100 years old, and extremely haunted. The activity in my home started me on a journey to find others that have also experienced the Paranormal.

I've touched on some of my experiences in the home I grew up in through my other books. My parents still live in that same house today, and the paranormal activity continues. My wife, my children, and I, all have experiences in the home from time to time. My parents and brother, who live in the house, share their new experiences with me on a regular basis.

My Father's Experiences

One afternoon I received a call from my dad. He explained that he had two experiences in the home in the last week that were very unusual. One night he woke up to a strange blue light on the ceiling above his bed. He put on his glasses to figure out what was projecting the light, and as he did, he realized it wasn't on the ceiling at all. It was a ball of light that hung just below the ceiling. As he watched, it started to dance and move about through the air above the bed. He watched, mesmerized until it disappeared in a flash and was gone. He laid back in bed and went back to sleep, wondering what this new phenomenon was.

A few days later, my father got up in the middle of the night and sat in the front room in his chair (as he often does), trying to get a little more sleep. He had been sitting in the front room for a few minutes when he heard a sound come from the kitchen. He jumped up to see if my mother or brother were up, but when he got to the kitchen, no one was there. He flipped off the light and turned to go back to the front room and came face to face with a man. The man was short, only about 5 feet tall. He had dark hair, and he was only a foot away from my father's face. My father jumped back and flipped on the kitchen light, but the apparition had vanished. The vision of the short man, however, was burned in my father's mind.

My Personal Experiences

A few months ago, I stopped by to visit my Mother and Father on a Tuesday afternoon before picking up my youngest son from school. As I walked in, I called out "Hello!" and was greeted back by a typical "We're in Here!" I walked through the kitchen and into the front room to find no one was there. Confused, I walked around the house calling out but could find no one home. I walked out to the kitchen, and when I looked out the window, I noticed my parent's car was not in the garage. At this point, I heard someone in the sitting room behind me laugh. I turned and walked towards the laugh, and again, I found no one in the house. At this point, I knew it was the ghost we call The Stair Monster playing tricks on me, so I sat down to watch tv and waited for my parents to come home.

After about a half-hour, I heard the back door open, and my father called out, "Hello!" I yelled back and got up to go to the kitchen to see if my parents needed help bringing anything in from the car. But as I walked into the kitchen, I was met with silence. I walked to the window again and could see the garage was still empty. At this point, I once again heard someone laugh from behind me. I shook my head and said out loud, "You got me again!"

I went back into the front room. After about 15 minutes, I heard the back door open, and a voice yell out, "Hello!" This time I just sat and continued watching TV. After a few more minutes, my dad walked into the front room. "Didn't you hear me call?! I could have used some help with the groceries!" I laughed and told him what had happened.

My Wife's Experiences:

About a year ago, my wife and I sold our house, and were trying to find another home that was farther out of town…something a little quieter. We had planned on renting during our search, but my parents asked if we wanted to stay with them for a month while we looked for a new home. We thought this might be a great idea. Not only would it help out my parents but it would also help us to save a month's rent, so we agreed. My wife, who has experienced a few of the Stair Monster's noises at the house, was a little concerned about the activity. I explained I would let the Stair Monster know she was not ok with his antics and ask him not to frighten her. She reluctantly agreed, and we moved into the upstairs bedroom and settled in. The first three weeks were enjoyable, and we had no paranormal activity that affected either of us.

At the end of the third week, we had found a new home, and our offer had been accepted. We were about a week from moving out of my parents' home when my wife mentioned that she was surprised nothing out of the ordinary had occurred. I looked at her and said in a loud mocking voice, "Well if you're ok, I'm sure the Ghost wouldn't mind letting you know he's here." She gave me a light punch on the shoulder, and we went back to our packing.

The next morning, I got up very early, dressed, and headed to work. My wife had just fallen back to sleep when she felt someone slide into bed and snuggle up next to her. . She woke, feeling someone running their hands through her hair. At first, she thought it was me, but quickly the realization hit her. I had already left for work. She jumped out of bed with a yell and turned on the light to find she was all alone in the bedroom. She stood there shocked, trying to catch her breath when she heard a quiet giggle come from the corner of the room. She threw her clothes on quickly and headed downstairs.

The last week we were there, the Ghost made up for lost time. He consistently let her know he was around by knocking on the door now and then, having a little laugh at her when she went to look for something that had gone missing. He would also sometimes poke her lower legs as she was

4

getting dressed. Needless to say, my wife was thrilled to be moving into our new home at that point.

Other People's Experiences

When I started interviewing people for Book 3, I found so many beautiful people willing to share their stories. This book covers Utah, Idaho, Wyoming, Oregon, Washington, and Nevada. I've been able to travel and meet so many great people. It's so beautiful to get to know each of them. If it weren't for all those willing to let me share their experiences in the world of the Paranormal, I would not be able to share these books with you. This book is really about them. I sincerely hope you enjoy these stories. Just like in my other books, please keep in mind I take all my stories from first-hand accounts. I only collect stories from the people who actually experienced them. I feel so blessed to be able to share them with you.

Sincerely,

John Olsen
Author "Stranger Bridgerland Series.

Old Main

From Julie

In the early '90s, I got a job working for Utah State. My job was to clean and help with maintenance at the Old Main building. Growing up, I'd had a few experiences with the supernatural. The home I grew up in was haunted, and I had a strong belief in the paranormal.

My first few months at my new job were uneventful. I started at 4 am and would clean and straighten up whatever was on the list of things to do. I felt comfortable in most parts of the old building. However, there were a few places that gave me the creeps if I went in there alone. The old library on the 3rd floor was one of those places. If I was working up there, I always felt like someone was watching me. I also felt occasional cold spots, they felt like an icy wind that blew right through you.

My first real paranormal experiences happened early one morning as I stepped off the elevator into the basement. As the elevator doors closed, I turned to walk down the hall towards the vending machines. I was surprised when I saw a lady at the end of the hallway walking towards me. As I got closer, I could see she was wearing clothes that were very old fashioned. She had on a gray blouse with a tan fabric belt and a long dark skirt. Her brown hair was up in a bun with some strands that had fallen out like she had been hard at work on something. As we passed in the hall, she looked up, smiled and politely said, "Hello," I thought I knew everyone working in the building, and she wasn't anyone I knew. Later I asked my coworkers if they had seen her? They explained that I had seen the "Lady in Gray," a ghost that many people have seen in the basement of Old Main.

Over time, as I worked at Old Main, I saw the "Lady in Gray" several times. She was never scary and always busily going from place to place in the basement.

Another of the ghosts I encountered in the time I worked there was a gentleman on the 3rd floor. There were many times I would walk around the corner, or exit a room on the 3rd floor, and see him at the end of the hallway facing away from me. He was an older man in late 1800's suit, and as you approached, he would always walk around the corner and disappear. I never saw his face because he was always facing away from me, and he was always standing close to a corner of the hall. As you approached, he would simply slip around the corner. No matter how fast you got to the turn, he would be gone.

I worked there for just under a year before I moved on to something else. But during that time, I had many experiences that I will never forget. I never felt threatened or perceived an evil presence, but I left knowing the building was alive with the spirits of the past.

Haunted in Boise

From Jenna

I moved to Boise in the early 2000s. I grew up in Oregon and had finished college in Washington. I was looking for a fresh start, and so I found a Job in Boise that would put my new IT degree to use. I wanted out of all the hustle and bustle of the bigger cities in the Northwest. I wanted to be close enough to home that I could drive to see my family but also far enough away that they wouldn't drop in unexpectedly.

I had stayed in an apartment for my first year. I loved Boise so much that I decided I wanted to stay and put down roots. I started looking around town hoping to find a little house I could make my own. I found a few places I liked but wasn't finding anything that was within my budget. I was almost ready to quit when I came across a house on the east side of town that I fell in love with. It was on the small side, and it needed some love, but I was excited to make it my own. I put in my offer, and to my surprise, it was accepted. I was ecstatic to finally be a homeowner and have a place to call my own.

I closed on the house and moved in the next day. I didn't have a ton of stuff, so it only took a day with a little help from some friends to move in. The first night in my new house was so exciting! The friends that helped me move stayed over that first night. We talked, played games, and had a blast! I moved in on a Friday afternoon, so I had the whole weekend to get everything put away and get everything in the home just right.

It was a few weeks before I noticed anything unusual about the house. One day, I was in the kitchen rinsing off some dishes and looking out the window at the neighbor's dogs lost in my thoughts, when suddenly, some movement to my left caught my attention. I looked up just in time to see the cabinet slowly open up. As I stared at it, confused, trying to figure out what was happening, it slammed shut with a; "BANG!"

I jumped back and let out a yell. It had completely taken me by surprise, and the sound it made when it shut was so loud. I caught my breath and walked over to the cabinet door. I inspected it, trying to figure out what caused it, but I couldn't find anything wrong with it.

The more I thought about it, the more I was just confused. It was an old house, maybe the walls had shifted, or there was a breeze that had come through. I tried to rationalize what I saw. But finally, I shook it off as a one-time thing and decided to move on.

Up until this point, I had never really thought ghosts were a real thing. I had spent my entire life thinking that people who believed in the paranormal were imagining things they wanted to be true, or that they were probably seeking some attention. Little did I know I was about to have that theory turned upside down. I would soon find out for myself that ghost and the paranormal can be very real.

About a week later, I was in front of the house, reading in my little sitting room. I was deep into my book when I felt a strange feeling come over me. It was a warm summer afternoon, but all of a sudden, it felt frigid in the front room. I started getting the feeling that I was being watched. I grabbed the comforter by the couch and sat back down and got ready to curl up and get back to my book.

As I turned to grab my book off the end table, some movement caught my eye. When I looked up, I saw an old woman standing there in the entrance to the living room. She was wearing a housecoat over a flowered pajama dress. As I looked at her, I realized she was staring at me through angry eyes with a snarl on her face. I was in shock! I was about to yell at her to get out of my house when she took a step towards me and vanished before my eyes. I jumped up off the couch and ran out of the house.

I was so frightened! I stood on my lawn for a few minutes, trying to go over what had just happened. I was trying to remind myself that I didn't believe in ghosts...or at least up until that moment I didn't. But here I was, standing on my front lawn afraid to go back to my house. After 15 minutes or so, I ran into the house, grabbed my keys, and drove off. I drove to my friend Tammy's apartment. I explained what had happened, and she let me spend the night with her. I was still afraid to go home the next day. I didn't know what to do. Tammy agreed to spend that next night with me at my house. I knew I couldn't abandon my home, but I also wasn't sure what I was dealing with.

Tammy spent a few nights with me, and nothing out of the ordinary happened. Slowly, I got back to my everyday life. Before long, I forgot about the incident and figured I must have just imagined it.

About a month later, I awoke at 3 am on a Sunday. I wasn't sure what woke me, but when I rolled over to go back to sleep, there she was. The old woman was back! She was staring at me from a chair I had placed in the corner of my room. It was dark, but the light from the street showed in through the window. It was just enough light to allow me to make out all her details. Her glare was angry, just as it had been before. I froze in my bed. I couldn't move. I was so scared! After what felt like forever, I got enough courage up to close my eyes and throw the covers over my head. I'm not sure how long I stayed under my covers, just shaking with fear. After some time, I peeked out, and the woman had vanished. I ran to the front room. I turned on all the lights and the TV. I sat there shaking until the sun came up.

I after that night, I was determined to find out what I need to do to get rid of this menacing ghost. This was my house, and I wasn't leaving! I did some research and found out that the old lady who had lived there before me had died a month before I purchased the home. She had lived there for 30 years before she was taken to an assisted living facility. The family had removed all her things from the house and rented it out until she had passed away. At that point, her family decided to sell the house, which is when they had sold it to me.

I researched information about cleansing my home. When I talked to my friend about what I was trying to do, she suggested that I speak to an acquaintance of hers; Spencer. Spencer had gone through something similar to me. I met with him, and he suggested that I should speak to the ghost out loud. I should say to the spirit that it was my house, and I wasn't going anywhere. He also suggested that I express to her that I was sorry for how her family treated her, but it was my house now. He explained he had done this with his home and it had worked. He didn't have any problems after trying this.

During my research of the house, I found out that in life, her name had been Debra. What I was about to do went against all my beliefs. I was about to talk to someone that was not alive, someone that literally wasn't standing in front of me, and yet her presence was. I felt ridiculous, but I was at my wit's end. I didn't know what else to do. So, I walked into my house and called the Spirit by name. I told Debra in a stern voice this was my house, and that I was not leaving. Just as Spencer suggested, I told her I was sorry for how her life had gone, but that this was my house now. I did this same thing several days in a row, and things seemed to get better.

Things went back to normal for a few months until one evening I was sitting watching TV when I heard some of the cupboards open and shut loudly a few times in the kitchen. I got up to see what was going on and found nothing. I went back to the front room, and as soon as I sat down, I heard the cupboards open and shut again. I knew I needed to deal with the situation. I mustered up all the strength I had, and trying not to sound frightened, I said, "Debra! This is my home now. You can't go around messing things up. Please leave me be!" The sounds stopped, and a calm feeling came over me.

I spent five more years in that house before I sold it, I never had another problem with Debra.

Center Street Ghost

From Travis

The home I grew up in is in an older part of Logan, Utah. It's an older home, and I still live there today. From the outside, it seems unassuming, but inside, it's a different story. My interest in the paranormal started because of the experiences I had while living in this home.

One of the strangest things that continue to happen has to do with a small child. I'll be sitting in my bedroom or the front room, and I get the feeling I'm being watched. As I look up, I'll see a young boy at the doorway peeking into the room. I barely catch a glimpse of him, it's just his head, and then he slips back through the doorway. Almost as if he is playing peekaboo with me. It only happens once in a while, but when he starts, he will do it over and over until I get up to leave the room.

As I mentioned, my experiences living in this house have sparked my interest in the paranormal. A while back, I began to purchase some equipment to do paranormal investigations both in and out of my home. I wanted to be able to gather proof of what I was experiencing.

One evening, after I had started investigating haunted places, I heard things moving in my hallway. Even though I knew I was all alone in the house, I kept hearing someone's footsteps out in the hall. I never had a reason to close the door when I sleep so I could hear the footsteps very clearly. I happened to have my thermal camera next to my bed, so I turned it on and pointed it toward my open bedroom door. As I looked down at the screen, I could see the faint outline of a tall skinny man in the doorway. His shape was eerily outlined by the fact that his temperature was so different than the rest of the room. He seemed to be standing still, staring at me from the hallway just outside my door. After a few moments, he walked off. I jumped up and headed into the hall. I turned on the light and searched the house, but as I suspected, I was all alone.

On more than one occasion, I've been in the house and seen a young lady in older period clothes. She has short red hair and an old-style 1800's dress. I usually see her when I am walking into a room. I walk in just as she walks out the door on the other side of the room. I always rush over to try and get a better look, but she is never there, and I'm alone in the house. It's always the same, I walk into one side of a room, and she is walking out the other. There have been other times when I have been sitting in my bedroom, and she walks by my window. I'll rush outside but never find anyone around. She seems to like that side of the house and the front room for some reason.

I've had some success catching EVPs in my home. One that I've been able to pick up is the voice of an older man. He seems to be upset I live there. I set a recorder up in my bedroom. Later, as I sat back listening to it, the recording was quiet for a long time. Then out of the blue, a deep clear voice said sternly, "Get out!". I sat bolt upright. I couldn't believe what I'd heard. I played it over and over; it was definitely the voice of an old man forcefully telling me to leave.

I still live in the house, and I am sure I will for a long while. I'm not afraid to live here, but I am very excited to see what's next.

The Cloaked Vision

From Keven

I was born and raised in northern Utah. I spent my entire life hunting and fishing in the Cache National Forest. I know the woods of Cache Valley like the back of my hand. I spend most of my downtime driving in the wilderness and exploring all of northern Utah. One August day, I packed a lunch, loaded up my Jeep, and headed for the mountains East of Logan Utah. Except for a couple of bow hunters, I saw no one else as I spent hours driving up the rough mountain roads.

As the day went on, I found myself in an area that always seems to give me the creeps. Despite that, it's a beautifully serene area at the very top of the mountains. Thick with massive pines, and eerily quiet. You constantly feel as though you are being watched whenever you are in the area. I parked my Jeep and spent some time walking around.

Once again, the feeling of being watched crept over me. I sat quietly but didn't hear or see anything. My only companion was that deep-seated feeling I was not alone. I walked back to my Jeep and unpacked my lunch and ate, sitting in my vehicle.

I had almost finished my lunch when something caught my eye to the right side of my Jeep. Something I couldn't explain was running down the hillside towards me. The best way to describe it was that it looked almost cloaked like I was looking at it through a heat mirage. I got the distinct feeling that I was looking at Native American running down the trail at me, but as though he was partially hidden in a cloaked haze. The figure ran past the front of my Jeep, not more than a few feet away. Then cloaked figure crossed the road in front of me and continued down the path on my left and disappeared. I sat in stunned silence, waiting for it to return. However, it did not.

After a while, I started up the Jeep and headed home. The experience left me confused and excited. I'm not sure what it was I saw that August afternoon, but to this day I can still see it play out in my mind like it was yesterday.

Growing up with Ghosts

From Nikki

My family moved to an older home in Hyrum when I was 8 years old. For a while, everything seemed just fine. After a few months, it almost seemed as if someone opened a portal to the "other side." Our lives were turned upside down.

I would wake up at night to strange sounds. Footsteps and disembodied voices became commonplace. It wasn't just me, everyone in the house started having experiences.

My dad would often wake up in the middle of the night and find the TV turned on at full volume in the front room. Each time, he would turn it off and check the house, only to find everyone asleep. All the doors and windows were shut and locked, just as he had left it when he'd gone to bed.

Other times my parents would wake up to the sound of the faucets in the kitchen or bathroom running at full blast. They would check, once again, however they always found everyone asleep and no one in the house.

My mother can recall many occasions where she could hear footsteps upstairs on the 2nd floor after we had all left for school. She would call out, but no one ever answered her. If the sounds continued, she usually went upstairs to see who was home. But it was the same every time, the was house empty.

When I got to be teenager, I started to wear headphones at night. Then I could listen to music instead of the footsteps and voices that would consistently be in the hallway at night. On a few occasions, I had my headphones in and had fallen asleep only to be awoken abruptly by the ghost. It had learned to turn the volume up on my radio or change stations to a loud song to get my attention.

There were times when I would be working on something in my room, when suddenly I could hear someone clearly call my name. Sometimes I would call back but get no response. Other times I would go looking for whoever called me but would find that I was alone, or that no one in the house had called my name.

One afternoon my boyfriend and I were upstairs watching TV and spending time together. I needed to go downstairs to use the restroom, so I jumped up and told him I'd be right back. I walked downstairs, turned the corner, and walked towards the bathroom. As I walked through the living area, I glanced at the large mirror we had on one side of the room. There, standing behind me, was a figure. My first thought was that it was my boyfriend. I turned to give him a snide look and tell him he had succeeded in scaring me, but there wasn't anyone there. I turned back to the mirror and saw a young man standing behind me in the mirror. I stood there for a few seconds, shocked. As I calmed down, I began to look closer. I could see it was a young guy, he was short and very stocky. He was probably in his early 20's, and he had an orange tinge to him, almost like I was looking through an orange filter at him. He looked at me for a few more seconds and then turned around to walk into the room behind me. Only then did I realize that he was only visible from the waist up. I stood staring as he walked into the room right behind me and disappeared. I turned and ran upstairs.

One night in my late teens, I was in my bed; almost asleep. I had my door open and was about to put on my headphones when I heard a terrible fight going on in the hallway. It sounded like two people screaming at each other. My first thought was that it was my parents. But after listening for a few seconds, it didn't sound like them. As I got up and ran towards my bedroom door, I heard a woman scream! As I carefully approached the hallway, I heard someone run past and seemed to trip and fall as they passed my door. I heard a horrible thud as if a body had just hit the floor outside my door. Scared to death of what I had just heard, I walked into the hall. I expected to see a body laying on the floor outside my room, but as I got there and looked, I found nothing. I turned on the hall light but there was absolutely nothing. Silence filled the house as I walked around, looking for any foul play. I honestly expected to find a body, blood, or something. But I only found silence. Everyone was asleep in their beds, and there were no signs of a fight or any indication that anything was wrong at all. I felt a cold creepiness pass through me as it moved down the hall, so I shut my door and jumped back into bed. I laid there, wide awake for what seemed like forever. I strained listening for any more noises, but I heard nothing. After a long while, when I was reasonably sure everything was gone, I put in my headphones and finally fell asleep.

I have since grown up and moved out of the house. My parents no longer live in the home either. I often think of asking the current owners if they have had any experiences, but how would you start that conversation? I've had a few paranormal experiences in other places I've lived, but nothing has come close to the frightening things I experienced as a child and young adult living in that house in Hyrum.

Cadillac of Fear

From Teri

At the time of the occurrence, I lived in Hyde Park, Utah. At that time I was visiting a friend that lived in Smithfield. I had spent the evening hanging out and watching shows with my friend when I realized it was already 2 am. I knew I had things to do the next day, so I quickly said my goodbyes and headed out the door.

I jumped in my car and started it. I sat and waited a few minutes for my car to warm up, and then I was good to go. I backed out of the driveway, checking both ways to make sure the road was clear. There was no movement anywhere on the road, so I backed out onto the shoulder of the road. I checked all my mirrors and still didn't see anyone. With the streetlights, I could see down main street for at least 2 or 3 blocks. It was a weeknight, so I wasn't expecting to see anyone else out on the road at 2 am.

I pulled left out into the median and rechecked both ways. It was clear, with no cars. I turned and headed south towards home. Just as soon as I had merged onto the left lane, bright headlights illuminated my vehicle. It scared the life out of me! I jumped and looked in my rearview mirror to see a car right behind me with its high beams on. I was frightened and a little confused, because just a few moments earlier, there were no cars to be seen. With or without its lights on, I would have seen this car when I pulled out. I slowed down and moved into the outside lane to let them pass, but the car just slowed down and pulled in behind me.

I was starting to get very upset. I had no idea who would be out at this time of the morning and still had no idea where the car had come from. After another couple seconds, the vehicle shut off its high beams and I got a better look at it. It looked to be an old Cadillac, and as we passed under a streetlight, I could tell it was bright red. I found it to be very odd that someone would be out at this time on a weeknight in an old Cadillac. I thought it was also strange that with the entire road to ourselves, he was following so closely behind me, scaring me to death! I tried to get a look at the driver from my rearview mirror but I couldn't make out a face, it was just a dark outline of the driver.

As I speed up, the car behind me would also speed up. If I slowed down so it could pass, it would stay behind me and also slow down. I looked back again at the car as we passed under another street light, trying again to get a better look at the driver. To my shock, the Cadillac had changed colors. It was now white, and the driver had a glow all around him.

I was terrified at this point and sped up, but the car just kept pace right behind me. When I looked back again, the car had changed from plain white to a glowing white. The entire car and driver had an intense, bright glow all around it. As the brightness increased, it got hard to look directly at the car.

I was almost 90 mph at this point. I knew I was speeding. I was hoping I'd run into a cop or someone that could help me, but no one was around except me and the glowing car.

I knew I was coming up to my turn soon. I was wondering what to do when suddenly, the bright light behind me went out. I looked in my rearview mirror, and the car was gone. I couldn't see anything but an empty street and the pockets of light that the street lights cast down in the distance. I slowed down and made my turn. As I did, I looked expecting the Cadillac to reappear, but there was nothing behind me. I was still nervous as I drove the rest of the way home. I pulled in the driveway, and as quickly as I could, I sprinted for the door. Once I was inside, I leaned against the closed door, stopped to catch my breath, and tried my best to calm down. After a minute or two, I looked out my window but couldn't see anything.

As time has passed, I think back and still, wonder what it was that followed me that night. I know it wasn't a typical car. I genuinely believe that whatever it was, it wasn't from this world.

Dark Places

Author Notes:

I grew up loving the outdoors. When most kids were skipping school to go hang out or go to the mall, I was playing hooky to go fishing, hiking, or hunting. I spent most of my life in the wilderness of Utah, Idaho, and Wyoming. In my vast adventures in the wild, I've come to find that almost anything can hold emotions and spirits. Homes, buildings, canyons, mountains even object can be haunted. If something has happened in a place, such as a traumatic event or death, it can taint an area, this includes the wilderness.

I have had experiences where I have walked into spaces, whereas soon I entered, I felt as though something sucked all the air from my lungs. I've also been in areas where I've become instantly overwhelmed with sadness, fear, or anxiety. There are also places I have gone where I get a deep-seated feeling in my gut that tells me I am not welcome there. People call them many different things, but I call them dark places.

The story you're about to read is about one of those places. I've been to this canyon both on a day hike and at night. It's a popular place to camp. Others people I know have gone there and haven't had any issues. I personally wouldn't go there alone, especially at night.

From Austin

It was the late 90's, some friends I and from school decided we were going to go camping. It was late spring, and Left-Hand Fork up from Blacksmith Fork above Hyrum Utah had just opened for the season. We were all just about to finish up our Junior year in high school.

It was a warm spring Friday. We loaded up my truck and headed up towards Left hand. We didn't have a specific camping spot in mind but figured we would know it when we saw it. As we drove, we passed a lot of other campers. But the further we got out in the wilderness, the fewer people we saw. By the time we decided to stop, we hadn't seen another campsite in quite a while. We stopped at the bottom of a canyon that I would later find out was called Bear Hollow. We set up camp and gathered enough firewood for the night. We got the fire going and talked a while, and a few of us went fishing.

After dinner, the sun went down, and we sat around the fire telling stories until midnight. At that point, one of my friends suggested a night hike. We grabbed our flashlights, and the four of us headed up Bear Hollow towards the north. We were talking and laughing as we hiked. But, as we continued up the canyon, I started to get a little anxious. I couldn't pinpoint what was bothering me. Something in the back of my mind just knew; something wasn't right. As we hiked up Bear Hollow, it seemed to get more and more creepy. There were cliffs and rock faces on both sides of us, and I started to feel trapped. I noticed everyone had stopped laughing and talking. It's as if we all felt a dark presence looming over us from all sides.

No one wanted to be the guy that wimped out. So no one suggested we go back. We just kept walking the trail. I had a definite feeling we should turn around and go back to camp. Somehow I ended up at the front of the group. I was shining my light up the path ahead. Still feeling very uneasy, I finally couldn't take it anymore and turned to my friends and said, "Hey guys, let's head back." My friend Tim suggested we walk just a little further around the next corner or two.

I reluctantly turned and continued to head up the trail. We were approaching a spot where the path wound around a cliff when my light caught some sort of movement just ahead near the bend. I stopped and shifted my light towards the area to see if I could get a better look.

Everyone stopped next to me, straining to see what had made me stop. I could see what looked like a dark shadow just past the edge of the cliff and then caught some movement again. I was just about to ask if anyone could see what I was seeing. But before I could speak the words, a large dark shadowy hand reached around the cliff. It was followed by the shadow of a giant head. It appeared that whatever it was, it was peeking around the side of the cliff. It was extraordinarily tall. The pitch-black shadow figure was about 20 yards in front of us, staring directly at us from behind the cliff face.

My mind had just begun to register what I was seeing. I came back to my senses when I heard the pounding footsteps of my friends. They were heading as fast as they could down the canyon. I quickly realized I was standing there all alone. I turned on my heels and ran after them as quickly as I could. I have never been more afraid in my entire life. As I ran, I could hear my heart pounding in my ears. Not just because I was running, but because I was terrified!

We didn't stop running until we arrived back at camp. We were all sucking in air and trying to catch our breath; our lungs burning. I was astonished that I hadn't tripped on the path as fast as I had run back to camp. We stoked the fire as big as we dared, and talked about what we saw. We had all seen the same thing, a large black hand followed by a blackhead standing at least 10 feet tall, peeking around the cliff at us.

I really wanted to go home that night, but I wasn't going to be the one to say it. I'm sure I wasn't the only one that felt that way. Just like when we were walking through the eerie canyon, no one wanted to be the guy that was going to chicken out. So instead we sat by the fire, more scared than we cared to admit, unable to sleep. We huddled around the fire all night, talking to each other to stay awake.

After thinking about it and doing some research over the years, I've come to believe that what we saw that night was a shadow person. I don't know why it was there. But retelling the story of that night still scares me, even when I think of it today.

Hotel from Hell

From Jerod

I grew up in Eastern Idaho, but when I was 21, I moved away from the family farm and went searching for my new life in Oregon. I spent about a year and a half working in Eugene. I'd been searching for a new way of life, and the 60's counter culture was very prevalent in Eugene. This was a significant change coming from Eastern Idaho.

During my short time in Oregon, I found Jen, the love of my life. We had been dating for about six months when my brother called to tell me my father had died. He and I hadn't always seen eye to eye, but he was my Dad, I loved him just the same.

At the funeral, my brother asked me to move home and help him with the farm. He only needed help for a year so he could save up the money to hire a crew to help run it. Growing up, I hated the farm and had my whole life. But I loved my older brother, and I knew how much the farm meant to him and my Mom. I decided to quit my job and move back for a year. It killed me to leave Eugene and to leave Jen. We were not in a place where I could ask her to marry me or move for me, but I felt the relationship was really going somewhere. I was determined to do my best to call regularly and travel to Oregon as much as I could to visit her.

It was a late October by the time I was able to get to Oregon to see Jen. We spent the weekend together and had a great time. I hadn't seen her in a month. I'd missed her, and I really enjoyed being able to spend time with her. I promised my brother I'd be back by Tuesday at the very latest, so I left Sunday evening and headed back towards the farm.

I'd been driving a couple of hours when I blew a tire in my old 1959 Chevrolet Biscayne. I changed the tire and got going again. I drove for another hour and stopped in a small town not far from the Idaho border. Being up late hours over the weekend and then the effort of fixing the tire had really taken its toll. Exhaustion was setting in, and I knew it would be a better decision to stop and sleep than to try and drive the rest of the night. I went to the old Hotel in town to see if I could get a room for the night. I remember thinking how strange it was that there were a lot of cars in the parking lot. There must have been something going on in town to have that many people staying at the local hotel.

I walked to the front desk to find a young man close to my age behind the counter. As he looked up, I smiled and asked, "Hi bud, I need a room for the night."

He looked up at me with a concerned frown on his face. "I'm afraid we are full. There is a funeral in town tomorrow, and there are a lot of people from out of town staying with us," he explained.

The need to sleep was even stronger now. "Is there anywhere else I can stay?" I pleaded.

With an apathetic look, he said, "No, it's a small town, I'm sorry."

I nodded and turned around to head out of the lobby when an older guy came around the corner from the back room. "Hello!" he called out. I turned towards him and nodded my head to acknowledge his greeting. "Where you off to?" he asked.

"I was headed to look for a room somewhere else." The older guy shot the young manager a stern glance, and the young guy got an angry look on his face. "Do you *have* a room?" I asked again, this time frustrated and confused.

The clerk looked at me, then back at the older gentleman. The older man nodded curtly and him and then walked off without another word.

The younger manager sighed deeply and waved me over. I wondered if it was just my looks. I had long hair and I found that sometimes there were places that didn't like giving people service if they looked rough around the edges. Some people can be quick to judge. If you were different, and not clean-shaven, they thought that maybe you wouldn't pay or might cause trouble.

I was perplexed because I'd never experienced that in Oregon, even eastern Oregon. I started to tell the clerk, "I can pay, and I'm not going to cause any trouble...," but the kid held up his hand to stop me.

"Look, I'm working the night shift tonight. I don't like getting up at 2 am to check people out." I started again to explain I needed the room till morning, but he waved me off with his hand to stop me from saying anything.

"The ONLY room I have is left #12, and when you come down at 2 am and want to be checked out, I'm going to be upset." I was really perplexed now, wondering what details I was missing here.

He continued, "So you're going to pay now, and you're not going to wake me up, OK!? If you want to check out, you will just leave the key at the desk. Got it!?"

I wanted to ask what was going on, but he seemed very upset, and I just wanted some sleep. Gratefully I nodded and said, "You bet." I filled out the registration, paid in advance, and got the key. I hauled the duffle bag out of my car and headed to my room. I was still trying to figure out why he thought I was only staying until 2 am. What was wrong with the room? What was wrong with him?

I opened the door and tossed my bag in the room as I looked around. It wasn't the most beautiful room I'd ever stayed in, but everything seemed just fine. Trying to forget about my confusion, I jumped in the shower. When I got out, I walked out into the room to find my duffle bag dumped out all over the bed. Puzzled, I checked the door, but it was locked and chained just as I had left it. I checked the windows; they

35

too were locked. I looked under the bed; nothing. I couldn't figure it out. I finally just shook it off, picked my stuff up, and put it back into my bag. I got dressed and shoved my duffle in the closet and headed out to find dinner.

There was a Diner nearby. It was nearly closing time, but the nice waitress let me order a salad. I almost fell asleep while I was eating my dinner. I walked back to the hotel, and as I walked past the front desk, the kid working the counter was locking up for the night. He refused to look at me, so I just passed by and headed to my room.

I unlocked my door, and the first thing I saw was my duffle thrown on the bed and the closet door wide open. I was now confused and annoyed. I looked around the room again and still couldn't see any way someone had gotten into my room without a key.

I walked down to see the front desk clerk. As I walked up to the desk, he had just grabbed a stack of papers and was headed to the back office. He saw me coming and rolled his eyes. I opened my mouth to talk, and he held up a hand to stop me. "Look, no one has a key except you. The only other key is the master key, and it's right here." He pointed to his keys on this belt. "No one has been in your room. I tried to stop you from staying in that room. My advice is to get as much sleep as you can." He pointed over to an old couch in the front lobby. "If at any point you still need sleep, but don't want to be in your room, you can sleep there." ...and with that, he was gone.

I was so confused but so exhausted at this point. I called my mother from the lobby to let her know where I was and briefly what had happened then headed to my room to go to bed.

When I got to the room, I threw my stuff on the floor and fell into bed. My head had just hit the pillow, and I was out. The next thing I knew my covers where being ripped off me. I jumped up with a start and turned on the lamp by my bed; nothing was there. I got up and checked the door, but it was still locked and chained. The covers were in a pile on the floor in front of the bed. I could see the entire room from where I was standing. I could see the room, bathroom and a closet and No one was in there but me. I checked the clock, and it said 11:00. I'd only been asleep about an hour. So, I climbed back in bed, still deliriously exhausted, and tried to fall back to sleep. Had I not been so tired, I may have left the hotel, but I really needed the rest.

I quickly fell into a deep sleep when, all of a sudden, I felt the bed move. I thought I was dreaming and was just about to fall back asleep when I felt someone grab my leg with a tight grip. I looked towards the end of the bed, and in the dim light, I could see the outline of a woman standing next to my bed. I could see she was in a white nightgown; she had long black hair and deep-set black eyes. She had a wound just above her left breast that was bleeding. Her face was contorted into an angry glare that cut right through me. It only took a few seconds to take this all in, but it felt much longer. I glanced towards the nightstand for just a moment to turn on the lamp. When I looked back, she was gone. I jumped out of bed in a cold sweat.

I knew I was not spending one more minute in that room. I threw my stuff in my bag and quickly got dressed. I ran down to the front desk and set the key on the counter. It was at this point I looked at my watch and saw it was 2:05 AM.

Everything the clerk told me now made perfect sense. I looked at the couch but decided to get back on the road. As I look back, I wonder who or what she was. She was in that particular room for a reason, whatever it was, she was furious about it. I've had a few brushes with the paranormal, but this one really shook me. I wish I could remember the name of that small town. I don't think the hotel would still be there but who knows...

Shadowed in Yellowstone

From Corey

This experience happened to me in Yellowstone Park in the early '80s, well before the big fire in 1988 wrecked the Park.

Growing up, I was a bit of a wild child. My dad drove an 18-wheeler and was always gone; my mom worked full time. Most of the time, my older brother took care of me, and he was not the best influence in the world. By the time I was in my teens, I was in trouble regularly.

My mother thought the scouting program would be good for me and that it might help straighten me out. She forced me to participate in activities with my troop, even though I detested it. The summer I turned 15, the scout group planned a high adventure to Yellowstone for a week. As soon as I heard about the trip, I told my leaders I wasn't going. But soon my mother also found out about the trip. She knew I didn't want to go, so she gave me a choice. I either I went to Yellowstone with the scouts, or I'd spend the summer on my Grandpa's farm in Montana instead.

There was only one thing worse than activities with the scouts, and that was Grandpa's farm. I hated that place. Whenever we visited, he would run us ragged. There was nothing to do in his little town, so to pass the time your only options were chores and more chores. I weighed my choices, and I reluctantly told her I would go on the high adventure with the scouts.

The Sunday before we left, I was still trying to find ways to get out of going. The other guys in the group disliked me, and the feeling was mutual. I didn't enjoy the outdoors; it just wasn't going to be any fun. I tried several different schemes, but needless to say, I did not succeed in getting out of the trip.

Monday morning we left from our small town just outside of Boise and headed towards Yellowstone. Feeling defeated, I laid down in the back seat of the old station wagon we were riding in and slept all the way there.

The first half of the week went just the way I expected, I already wished it was over. I just kept to myself as much as possible and read a book while the other boys fished and hiked. There were three leaders with us. The two older ones disliked me as much as the boys did. The third one was Tim, he was a younger guy in his 20's. Tim and I got along, ok. Sometimes I thought he was trying a little too hard. But, he still seemed to like me, and I was glad he was there. He felt like my only friend.

It was time for our big hike. We spent most of the day trekking up to a big lake, I believe it was somewhere on the north side of Yellowstone, but I'm not sure. Once we arrived, we set up camp. Most everyone headed off to fish, but I decided to hang out at camp.

That night we had dinner, listened to stories around the campfire, then headed off to bed. Each night we put our food up in a tree about 100 yards from camp. We were also instructed to never kept food in our tents at night because of the bears. We'd seen some bears begging by the road on the way into Yellowstone. We hadn't seen many as we hiked in, but we knew they were there.

The next night was Thursday, and the day had gone just like all the others. We finished dinner, then sat around the fire for a while telling stories and jokes. I was getting really tired of the stories, so I told my leader that I was going out to "use the woods." That was camp code for telling people you were leaving to go to the bathroom. I slipped away from the fire and walked about 100 yards away from camp out of sight of the fire and everyone that might see me. I slipped a cigarette out of my jacket and lit it up. I knew I'd be in big trouble if I got caught. When I think back, I believed I was quite the rebel. I was sitting there in the quiet night, and I remember the moon was full. I'd brought my flashlight, but didn't need it to see where I was walking.

I was sitting in the tress when I heard whispering coming from the brush. It seemed as though it was coming from all around me. It was very faint, and I couldn't make out what was being said. Then, I started to hear footsteps. I cursed under my breath and put out my cigarette. I figured it was some of the other scouts out to scare me, so I sat down quietly and listened. The whispering was on my left, and then it was on my right. It's tough to explain what I was hearing; it was a high-pitched whispering with almost a whistle in it.

I wasn't afraid because at this point I was convinced it was the other scouts. I sat still and continued looking around to try and see what was going on. Some movement in front of me caught my eye and turned my head to look at it. Walking towards me between two big trees was a massive, human-like figure that was entirely black. Its head, body, and limbs all appeared to be stretched out, making the character look very tall. The head wasn't round, but more like a long oblong shape. I froze as it started walking towards me. It reached a spot between the two trees and stopped. It was so tall!

As best I could tell, it appeared to be 8 or 9 feet tall, and it was solid black. If it's even possible, I would describe it as blacker than the night. With the moon being full, I could only make out its outline. Where I should have seen a face or clothes, I only saw jet black. I flipped on my flashlight and shined it towards the creature. When I did it completely disappeared from my view. I stood up and shined my light around the entire area, but it was gone.

I noticed then that the whispers had stopped too. I stood with the flashlight for a few moments in the quiet woods. The only sound I could hear was the pounding of my heart in my ears. I was just about to turn and head towards the campfire when the whispers start up again. I heard footsteps again, right where the creature had been walking before. At this point, I didn't wait to see it again, I turned on my heels and bolted back to camp at full speed.

When I arrived, I stood there, leaned over with my hands on my knees. Trying to catch my breath. When I stood up and looked around, everyone seemed on edge. I'd run in so quickly that everyone probably wanted to know what was wrong. I sat down for a few moments to gather my thoughts and continue catching my breath. I was trying to figure out how I was going to describe what I had seen. I was afraid the other boys would simply laugh and make fun of me.

Finally, Tim pulled me to the side, asked me what was wrong. I lost it. My voice cracked, and between the tears, I told him what had happened. I asked him not to mention it to the other boys. He promised he would keep it confidential, and we walked together back to camp.

Tim and the other leader walked down to the area where I told them I'd seen the creature. When they came back, Tim told me they hadn't seen anything, but the look in his eyes said to me that he believed me. When the other guys pressed him for answers, Tim told them I thought I had seen a bear. They said they'd gone out to check for it, but that I must have scared it off. They told the group not to worry. We all stayed up for a while longer, then went to bed.

I stayed closer to the group and to Tim for the rest of the week. It's hard to explain, but the combination of seeing that "thing," and the fact Tim believed the story about my encounter changed my life. I straightened up after that and decided to take school and life a little more seriously.

Seeing that creature near Yellowstone gave me an entirely new outlook on life. The notion that there could be paranormal things out there –like shadow people-- made life seem so much bigger somehow. It was a horrifying experience, but I'm glad I saw it. It helped shape me into the person I am today.

Sierra Wendigo

From Tyler

At the time of my encounter, I lived in Sparks, Nevada. It was the early 2000's and my girlfriend, and I worked in the casinos in nearby Reno. I was not fond of the outdoors, but my girlfriend Jill had grown up doing a lot of camping. Jill had been itching to go camping and finally talked me into going with her. We were both in our mid 20's at the time, and even though I wasn't In love with the idea of camping, I was very much in love with Jill, so I agreed to go.

It was easier for us both to take a few days off in the middle of the week since the weekends were the busiest times at the Casino. We decided to head west to the mountains. We stopped by my buddy's house to pick up all the camping stuff we needed. We borrowed a tent, sleeping bags, and a small cooking stove. It was the end of August, so most summer campers were already gone. We figured because it was the offseason and the middle of the week, finding a spot to set up camp wouldn't be a problem.

We loaded up, stopped off at the local Riley's grocery store, then headed west. I had no idea what I was looking for, but I figured Jill knew where she was going and would help us pick an excellent site.

After a couple of hours, and then about 45 minutes of driving on an old dirt road, we found a camping spot. We hadn't seen many people since we left the main road and we were well off the beaten path.

We unpacked, and I fumbled through setting up the tent with a little help from Jill. We made a fire and had some dinner. At this point, it was just after sunset, and the night was setting in. I noticed how absolutely quiet it was. At first, I thought maybe it was just me. I hadn't spent much time in the wild, and I assumed that there should be more noise.

Before I could say anything, Jill mentioned it seemed odd the bugs, and other forest sounds were missing from this place. I started to get a horrible feeling that we were being watched, but I had no intention of telling Jill. I was trying very hard to show her I was tough on this trip. I wasn't going to ruin my budding outdoorsman reputation by showing fear. We watched the fire and talked until around 10 then headed into our tent for bed.

As we lay in the tent, I still couldn't shake the feeling that we were not alone. I forced it out of my mind, and after I while, I drifted off to sleep.

I remember waking up to an odd sound. It sounded like someone was walking and dragging something. I listened intently hoping it was just a small animal, but as it got closer, I could tell whatever it was it was on 2 feet. I heard it shuffle into our camping area then stop. My heart was pounding so hard it felt like my chest was going to explode.

The moon was almost full, and so there was a lot of light shining down on our tent. Suddenly the steps slowly started again, this time towards our tent. I could just barely make out the silhouette of a figure on the wall of our tent. It had the shape of a man but seamed thin. It seemed tall and very skinny. It took a few more steps towards the tent and paused. I could hear raspy, almost sickly breathing coming from the creature. Each breath in sounded wheezy and strained. I slowly reached for the flashlight on my left side between my sleeping bag and the wall of the tent. When I grabbed it, I hit my water bottle with a loud clank. The deep breathing stopped. The sound must have scared it because the creature quickly jogged towards the trees.

My adrenaline kicked in, and I quickly jumped up and unzipped the tent door. I flipped on the flashlight and scanned across the campsite.

Everything seemed ok as I scanned across the site. Then, my light got to the spot in the trees where the creature had headed. There, standing next to one of the pine trees, nearly 30 feet away, was a sickly looking monster. It had one hand on the tree and one down by its side. It was 6 feet tall, and pale white. It looked like a pale sickly looking man,. He was facing away from me and not moving. It was almost as if he instinctively believed he was camouflaged if he stayed motionless. He had no clothes on and had very little hair. Just a few long thin black patches on his head. In the moonlight, I could see long fingers holding on to the tree on its left side. I could see each and every bone on this poor creature's body, it was terribly emaciated. I yelled out, "What do you think you're doing?!"

The creature slowly looked over its shoulder towards me, and I almost fainted. Its black eyes were sunken into Its head, lips pulled back menacingly from disgusting black teeth. It looked like a tall walking corpse. I let out a terrified scream, and the monster quickly shuffled off into the forest. It was at this point I realized that Jill was just over my shoulder. She began to sob asking. "What was that?" but I couldn't answer.

I pulled on my boots and hastily threw everything into the car. I broke the tent in the process of trying to take it down. At this point, I didn't care. I yelled at Jill to jump in the car, and we took off, throwing gravel behind us as I sped down the dirt road. I felt like I was still trying to catch my breath. Jill just kept repeating herself, "What was that? What was that?". I didn't answer because I just didn't know.

We drove for a long time. Lost in my own thoughts, I'd taken a wrong turn. I just wanted out of the woods! When we finally came to an opening in the forest, I stopped, wanting to make sure Jill was ok. We sat there holding each other and Jill just sobbed. After the sun came up, we were able to find our way back to the main highway. Needless to say, I never camped again.

Authors notes:

After some searching and a lot of questions with the witness, I believe what he and his girlfriend encountered was what the Native Americans refer to as a Wendigo. Wendigo is the Algonquian folklore name used in the Northeastern United States. There are echoes of this creature in native stories from all over North America.

Legend has it that the Wendigo is a creature created when an individual turns to cannibalism. It wanders the land, never able to adequately fill its need for food. Like many native creatures, it's not fully understood if it is a spiritual creature or a flesh and blood monster. Perhaps it remains stuck somewhere in between.

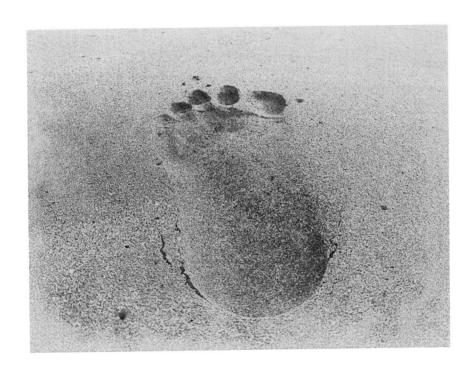

Little Foot

From Nikki

It was a beautiful Sunday afternoon when my (now) ex-husband and I decided to take a ride up in the mountains. I grew up in Cache Valley, and I still live there. One of my favorite things in the world is riding in the foothills in my Jeep.

I'm a big believer in the paranormal, but I hadn't given much thought to

Bigfoot. I'd seen Bigfoot shows on TV and heard stories here and there, but never thought I would ever see one.

We left home in the afternoon and headed up Logan Canyon. It is just east of Logan, Utah and runs 40 miles to Bear Lake. It's a beautiful scenic ride any time of the year.

We had reached the area called Peter Sinks located just to the west of Bear Lake. We drove all over the area and found ourselves on Swan Flat Road. It runs north, up towards the Idaho border.

It was starting to get towards dusk, and the animals were beginning to move around. We had seen a few deer here and there and some birds that we call Pine Hens. We had just come out of some dense trees. I looked to the east towards a stand of trees when I first saw it. It looked like a man dressed all in black, but as I looked closer, it was covered in thick dark hair. It was standing near a big pine tree and seemed very interested in us. I told my ex to stop the Jeep. With the jeep stopped, I got a little better look at it. It was about 5' tall and very muscular. It was completely covered in hair. I couldn't make out any distinguishing facial features, but I could tell it was staring right at us.

Suddenly, as if we'd done something to scare it, it leaped into the pine tree and scrambled to the top in a flash. I was amazed at how fast it climbed. It seemed to fly up to the top. It was huddled in the upper branches, and I could see that it was still staring at us. We watched it for a few more minutes as it started to get dark. We decided we didn't want to be around when it tried to come down. It wasn't till we pulled away that it clicked in my head, it must have been a young bigfoot.

We talked about it all the way home. My ex thought it was probably just someone in a ghillie suit until it shot up the tree with such speed. We may never know for sure. But, whatever it was, it was just as interested in watching us, as we were in watching it.

Uinta UFO

From Pete

At the time, it was 1999. I was going to the University of Utah in Salt Lake City. It was summer, and I was enjoying a break from school. I stayed around town and was just working to earn some money before the fall semester started. My roommates and I had become great friends over the last school year, and we decided to take a camping trip into the Uintas. We'd heard all kinds of fun stuff about the area, and we were really excited to spend three days in the beautiful mountains relaxing.

I'd grown up in Colorado and spent a lot of time hiking and camping. Andy, one of my roommates, had also spent some time camping as a kid. However, our roommate Loren grew up back east and had never been much for the outdoors. He was more of a city kid.

We rented and borrowed what we needed for our trip and left on a Wednesday morning. We headed towards the west and after a couple hours ended up in the mountains west of Heber City, Utah. We had taken my old Toyota truck up the back roads. The goal was to end up as far from civilization as we could. We set up camp in the woods, there was a clearing nearby with a beautiful view of a valley with a dry creek running down the middle.

Once we were settled in, we went for a hike. We didn't venture too far from camp, but hiked the hills and trails nearby and just enjoyed the day. That first night was uneventful. We had dinner, watched the fire, and talked into the evening. We went to bed really late and slept late in the morning.

The next day we did some more hiking. We had to take special care of Loren. He wasn't really as comfortable as we were in the outdoors. During our hike, he had gotten a tick and was completely freaked out. After convincing him he didn't need to go to the hospital, Andy helped me hold him down as I burned the little guy out. After a few minutes and a lot of screaming, we got the tick out and got Loren calmed down. We spent the rest of the day just hanging out by camp and relaxing. It was great to be out of the city.

That evening we did a lot of the same things as the night before. We made dinner and stayed up late talking, watching the stars and fire. At about midnight, I put out the fire, and we headed to bed.

I was the last one in the tent. I had just gotten one of my boots off when the tent lit up with a bright white light. It was so intense that I yelled and jumped to my feet. Both Andy and Loren jumped out of their sleeping bags, and we all looked at each other. I threw my boot back on, and jumped out of the tent, followed quickly by my friends. The light, whatever it was, had turned off. I strained to see clearly as my eyes were trying to adjust back to the darkness. I looked up to see a large dark object gliding over the trees. I could only really see a faint outline against the starry night sky. I quickly walked out to the clearing, away from the trees to try and see what it was.

It was a massive aircraft of some type. It was a long cylinder shape with a blunt nose. It's hard to describe, but the back was almost shaped like a giant black tool of some sort. I watched as it glided over the trees and down into the small valley in front of me. At this point, Andy and Loren had joined me, and I asked if they were seeing what I was. They described it as a dark black metallic object. They also pointed out to me that it was utterly silent. We weren't hearing any sort of motor noises coming from the ship.

I started questioning whether this thing had been the source of that blinding light when all at once, a bright white beam came from under the ship and hit the mountainside just below our camp. This was no regular searchlight. It didn't flare out or get less intense as it got further from its source, it seemed more like a broad white laser beam.

The light periodically scanned the mountainside as the object glided silently across the valley. We stood amazed as this enormous object scanned the hillside. To me, it looked as though it was searching for something. As it reached the other side of the valley, the beam turned off once again, and the valley was dark. It was hard to see the object now. It had traveled a fair distance away, and its light was off. I could just barely make out the outline as it flew over the hill and was gone. We watched in silence for a bit longer but didn't see anything else.

We turned back towards camp, looking at each other in silence. We sat down by the cold fire pit and talked about what we saw. We had all seen the light, and we each gave our guesses as to what we thought it was or what it was doing. We all agreed it was doing a search, but none of us had any idea what it was looking for.

The rest of our week was uneventful; nothing out of the ordinary. This has been my only run-in with a UFO, but it opened my eyes to the possibility we are not alone. I don't know if it was a secret government object or something from out of this world, but I've never seen anything like it before or since.

Author Notes:

The Uinta mountains of Utah are very well known for their UFO's. Stories have passed down by generations far back as the early Native Americans. Stories have also been told by the first white settlers to this area. The Uinta Mountains are a place of wonder. Whether it's UFO's, Bigfoot, Ghosts, or Skinwalkers, there are many paranormal stories to be found about this area.

Black Eyes at the Station

From Andrew

My encounter happened in the early 2000s. I had never had any encounters with the unknown in my life until this strange night. This meeting left me questioning my belief in the paranormal.

At the time, I was a consultant living in Boise, Idaho. The company I worked for had me doing IT work many small branches all across the west. I would drive in (I never flew because my company was kind of cheap that way), spend a day or so setting up software and training the employees, then head home. It wasn't too bad because I only had to pay my own living expenses when I was home. All my food and sleeping arrangements were paid for when I was traveling for the company. I usually traveled away from home for 3 - 4 days then I would have 3 - 4 days off. It was the perfect job for me because I like to travel, and I loved to see the west.

It was early May, I had just finished up an implementation in a Bozeman, Montana. It was Thursday afternoon, my usual routine for that day would have been to go have dinner and a drink. Then generally on Friday's, I slept in and headed home midmorning, getting home around 5 pm. However, this time, my friends were going to visit me at home for the weekend from Seattle, and I wanted a day to prep the house and shop for the weekend. So, I packed my bags up Thursday morning and checked out of the hotel before going into work. After finishing for the day and saying my goodbyes, I hit the road.

It's roughly an 8-hour drive from Bozeman, Montana to Boise, Idaho, and I knew the road reasonably well. I planned to be back in Boise by midnight or 1 am. I hit a snag in my plan as I passed a town called St. Anthony, Idaho. Just as I passed the town, I got a flat tire. I got everything out to change it myself but found my spare tire was flat. Aggravated, I called for a tow truck, and they brought me back to St Anthony. After 3 hours, I was fixed up and headed on my way. My next stop was Idaho Falls. I thought about stopping there for the night, but I wasn't exhausted. So I gassed up, grabbed a coffee, and got back on the road. Looking back, I regret not stopping for the night.

I would have generally stayed on the freeway headed south, but the gentleman who fixed my tire and told me had heard on his radio that there was an accident just past Blackfoot. So, I decided to take Highway 20 West. I had driven it before, and I knew the way without needing a map. The speed was slower, and I knew I needed to watch my gas gauge because there are fewer gas stations along that route, but I knew I didn't want any further delays. Highway 20 travels through some very rural areas and passes just north of Craters of the Moon National Park.

It was getting close to midnight, and I was starting to get low on fuel. I couldn't remember when the next gas station was coming up. I was beginning to get a little nervous when I finally saw a sign for gas station coming up. I pulled in and saw the store was closed. Luckily the pumps were on, so I pulled in. I started the pump and walked around a bit to stretch my legs. I was starting to get really tired and knew I wanted to push through to home, so I walked over to the pop machine in front of the store to look over my options.

It was a tranquil and cool night. As I looked over my drink choices, I got a strange feeling I was being watched. I looked up and just to the other side of the road to my left; I could see two small figures standing just off the road. They were just out of the range of the street lights so I couldn't see their faces or what they were doing. They just seemed to be standing there watching me. I quickly bought my pop and walked back to my car. I looked, but I couldn't see the figures from where I was pumping my gas.

I had just started to relax when I felt a chill behind me. I jumped as I heard a voice. It was a small girl about 8 or 9 - years old standing behind me. She was about 15 feet away, and I couldn't make out what she said. I turned and asked her, "I'm sorry, what did you say?".

She didn't look up, she was looking towards the ground at my feet, and she said, "Have you seen my mother?" I looked at her in surprise. She was wearing an old-style dress and had long dirty blond hair that covered her face. I should have felt some compassion, but instead, I had a feeling of complete dread come over me.

I told her, "No. I don't know your mother." I looked at the pump. I knew at a glance that I hadn't pumped enough gas to fill my tank, but I also knew I wanted to get out of their fast. I shut off the pump then quickly started to close up my gas tank. As I put the cap back on my tank, I looked up, and she was only about 6 feet from me now. This shook me because she had to have moved very fast and without me noticing at all.

"Can you help us find our mom?" she asked in a soft sweet voice.

"US?!" I questioned?

Just then, a boy around 11 – years old spoke up from the passenger side of my car. "Could you drive us up the road?" He asked.

As I looked at him, he also had dirty blond hair and older style overalls. They seemed genuine, and at the same time, really creepy and eerily calm. I was scared to death. I open my door and jumped in.

I started my car, then all the sudden the girl was at my window, tapping lightly on it with her fingernail. I was too freighted to even look at her.

I heard her say, "It's not far, please let us in."

I looked over at her, she was so close to me now, I finally got a little better look at her. Under her dirty hair, I could see her eyes were jet black. I shook myself out of a frightened trance, and I sped out of the station. I was too scared even to look back.

The rest of the drive was a blur. I made it home around 4 am. As I've thought back on the experience, I wondered what would have happened to me if I had taken the children. I'm not a big believer in dark beings, but whatever I experienced that night at the gas station was as close to evil as I ever want to come.

Little Green Man

From Aaron

I've only had one experience with the Paranormal, but that one experience was stranger than I would care to believe. To this day, I'm not sure what it was I experienced, but I do know, without a doubt, that it happened.

I was 15 at the time. I was the oldest, and I had 2 younger sisters and a younger brother. We lived in a 3-bedroom home, so I had to share my room with my younger brother, Sam. Being that Sam was the youngest, and I was the oldest, there was quite an age gap between us; 10 years to be exact. As you can imagine, at 15, sharing a room with a 5-year-old got a little annoying at times.

One morning I woke up with a start. I thought I'd had a vivid dream. As I sat there, for the next few moments, I couldn't think of anything but the dream...

...I had woken up in the middle of the night to the sound of Sam talking to someone. I had my back to Sam's bed, so I rolled over to see what was going on. My bed was on one side of the room, and Sam's was on the other. Between us was a small window that was up high on the wall. When I looked over at Sam, I could see him sitting on his bed and looking up at the window. Sitting on the window was a small man. This strange little man was about 2 feet tall, and he was wearing a suit and tie.

The suit was silver and shiny, and the little man had a green skin tone. There seemed to be a green hue all over him like he was glowing green.

I looked at Sam, and then the little green man. He smiled, politely at me and tipped his head like a bow.

Sam looked at me and said, "Aaron, you have to promise not to say anything. Do you promise?"

I looked up at the little man and said: "Sure, I promise,"…..

That's when the dream got hazy. I remember that the little green man told us both something, but I couldn't remember what he told us. Then I had fallen back to sleep or lost consciousness. The next thing I remember was waking with a start in the morning, recalling the vivid dream.

I looked at Sam as I sat in bed, trying to remember the last few details of the dream, but they still seemed confusing and hazy. Sam was still sleeping, so I got up and got ready for school. The rest of the day, my mind kept wandering back to the dream. I couldn't shake it. It was such a strange dream to me. I tried to remember what the little man had told me, but I just couldn't recall, no matter how hard I tried. I've had strange or vivid dreams before, but this one took the cake.

I finished up the day at school and headed home. After grabbing something to eat in the kitchen, I walked to my room to change clothes so I could go mow the lawn for my dad. When I walked into my room, I saw Sam was sitting on the floor, playing with his toy cars. I told Sam, "Hi." And started getting dressed. Sam's response to my greeting stopped me in my tracks.

Without looking up, he said, "Did you keep your promise?"

I looked at him and said, "What promise?"

He looked at me and then at the door and said in a whisper, "The promise not to say anything."

I couldn't believe what I was hearing, but I pressed him for more information. "What promise are you talking about, Sam?"

He looked a little annoyed at me. He jumped up and quietly shut the door, pulling on the knob to make sure it was shut. Then walked close to me and whispered, "Aaron, don't you remember the little man? The promise you made not to tell anyone?" He then pointed at the window sill where the little man had been sitting.

I looked at Sam in disbelief. I sat him down on the bed and asked him to tell me what the little man had told him. But Sam refused to tell me anything.

All that he would say was, "I promised not to say it to anyone."

I stopped asking questions, and he went back to playing. I was bewildered! I got dressed, mowed the lawn, and tried to explain it to myself. Was it a linked dream? Had I said something in the morning that Sam had overheard?

As time went by, Sam either forgot or decided to pretend not to remember. I never had an experience or dream-like it since. Many years later, when Sam was in his 20's, I asked him if he remembered it. He said that he felt like he'd a dream about a little green man in our window as a child, but it was way too fuzzy to remember. I decided to not push it for fear I'd seem like I was crazy. Even though I don't know what it was, I do know it was a strange experience that my brother and I shared.

Stairway to Nowhere

From Tom

I have spent all my life in the western states. Most of that time was in Utah, and there were a few years in Idaho. I'm in my 50's now, and I spend most weekends traveling to explore a new area. The west is a fantastic place to live if you enjoy the outdoors.

One weekend, when I was in my mid 20's, I packed up my backpack and loaded up my truck and headed out to explore. I was living in Logan, Utah at the time and usually, I would head either out to the west desert or up to the mountains. This weekend I was exploring part of the Cache National Forest. I had camped and hiked all over the valley and always enjoyed my time away from town. It was late afternoon on Saturday night, and I drove up Smithfield Canyon. I got out of my truck, threw on my small pack, and started to hike.

I had been hiking for about 2 hours. And the sun had started to dip low in the west. I was contemplating how long I wanted to hike and decided to hit a few more ridges before heading back. I came around a small peak when I noticed something extraordinary in front of me. There on the hillside was a set of stone steps. I walked over to them and found they were made out of rock. They were cut out of what looked like granite. I was perplexed. I was nowhere near a road or building, and they seemed to come out of a thick patch of brush and then up the slope above me. They were worn, but still very recognizably stairs.

I stood there, scratching my head, very confused. I decided to see where they went. I followed them up to the top of the next ridge about 100 yards up. At this point, it was starting to get dark. All at once, I had a strange feeling of dizziness come over me. I had to stop a few times and rest, which was not like me at all. As I approached the top of the ridge, I could see they continued on rising up through the mountain. They disappeared in the cliffs above. As I turned to go back, I noticed that I had a good look towards the valley below, but I realized I couldn't see anything to the west. At this time, it was almost dark, I should have seen the town, cars and other lights on below me but all that met my gaze was darkness.

As I stood there catching my breath, I had a deep-seated need to see where these stairs lead me. However, the darkness, dizziness, and increasingly creepy feeling I was having led me to abandon my search. I did my best to mentally map where I was so I could come back in the morning and find out where the stone steps would lead me.

I grabbed the flashlight out of my backpack and headed down the mountain. I left the stairs and cut back to the west. I knew that if I hit the ridge to my west, I could make my way back down to the main trail and find my truck. The trip back down should have been quick, but after a while, I started to lose my bearings.

After an hour, I crossed over to the next ridge and down. I made my way through some trees, and as I emerged, I could see the lights in the valley below. I rationalized that I had been too far east in the canyon to see clearly into the valley before. I made my way back to the truck and climbed in. I felt exhausted. I looked at my watch and was astonished to find it was only 11 pm. It was very confusing because it felt like I had hiked many more hours than that to get to my truck. It felt like 3 am; my body was just shaking from exhaustion.

I drove home and headed to bed. The next morning, I felt like I had run a marathon. I was in the best shape of my life, and the hiking the day before had not been hard enough to make me that sore. I thought maybe I was coming down with something. I spend all day Sunday in bed, and by Monday, I started to get my strength back.

It was a few weeks before I could get back to the Smithfield canyon when I did, I was utterly dumbfounded. I was able to find where I parked my truck and the path I had started on, but no matter how hard I tried, I couldn't find the stairs. I searched every weekend I could for a year but never found them. Even after I moved away, I would try to visit occasionally and spend a day hiking up there. But I never saw those strange stairs again. I've talked to many people who have spent time in Smithfield Canyon. And while there are many strange stories about that canyon, I've never spoken to anyone who came across my stairs. I often wonder what would have happened if I would have followed them to the end.

Black Eyes at 4 AM

From Alaina

My day started as usual at 3 am. It was 2015, and I worked at the Hospital in Logan, Utah. I lived in Smithfield, Utah, at the time, and I had to be to work at 4:30 am. I woke and got dressed and drag myself to the car. I pulled out and headed to the 7/11 for my morning cup of joe.

It was dark and relatively quiet as I pulled onto the main street and headed south. As I approached the light, I could see a figure crossing the road ahead. I slowed to a stop as the light changed for the person wanting to walk across the street. As I neared the intersection, I looked at the figure as he walked across the road. I could tell it was a young man around 14 years old. He had on a dark gray hoody, dirty Levis, and old sneakers. I could see he had long dark hair that covered his face as he walked with his head down.

All at once, an overwhelming feeling of dread and fear swept over me. I tried to shake it off, knowing I was perfectly safe inside my car. The kid hadn't done anything to show me he meant me any harm, but the fear was permeating me to my very core.

He finished crossing the road, the light turned green again, and I drove the last block towards the 711. I pulled in and jumped out to grab my coffee. As I walked towards the door, I scanned the street to see if I could see the young man. I couldn't see him anywhere.

I went in and fixed my coffee, paid for the cup, and headed for the door. As I stepped out towards the parking lot, there was the boy, sitting on the curb right by my car. He sat with his head down, and his long black hair still hanging down over his face. The fear shot through my body as the store's sliding door closed behind me. I froze for a moment, trying to figure out what to do next. My mind told me not to be stupid. He was a 14-year-old kid, and I was a grown woman. The logical side of me was saying, "Stop being such a wuss." But my inner soul was screaming out that this was wrong; VERY WRONG!

I took a sip of my coffee and walked to my car. I had to turn my back to him as I opened the car door to get in. I knew I had been quick to do it but was shocked to look up and see him now standing 5 feet from my car, facing me. His head was still down, and his hair was still in his face. The level of fear I had bubbling up inside me was something I had never experienced before.

I put the car in reverse and was about to back out of my parking spot when I took one more look at the boy. It was at this point he raised his head to look at me, and I gasped. Where I expected to see regular, maybe bloodshot eyes, I saw eyes that were dark black. His black eyes peered at me from a pale face framed with dirty black hair. I don't know how long I was staring at him, but I broke off eye contact and sped out of the parking lot. As I pulled out on the main street, I looked back one last time but couldn't see the young man anywhere.

I spent the next few weeks looking over my shoulder. His eyes came to me in my nightmares. I tried to explain what I had experienced to my friends, but no one really understood what I had felt or seen. Then one day, I was listening to a radio station when they brought up the Black-Eyed Kid's phenomena. Now it all made sense. They explained the other stories of people seeing them. I was happy to hear I wasn't alone in my experience.

Sasquatch Wakeup Call

From Chris

I live in a small town, north of Tremonton, Utah. My wife and I have both lived in the Box Elder area our entire lives. At the time it was in the late '80s, maybe 1988 if I'm not mistaken. I was working as a local driver, and I usually had to be up and going around 4 am, so I was generally in bed by 9:00 at the latest.

During the summer months it was tougher because the sun wasn't down when I needed to go to bed. It was also hard because we had the windows open after 9 pm so the house would cool down. So, sometimes there were noises outside as well. Luckily we lived on a dead end street. We didn't have many neighbors, just one across the street, there were mostly fields surrounding us, so even though the windows were open, it was reasonably quiet.

It was a quite summer night, and I had gone to bed early as usual. My wife had come to bed later, but I didn't remember her coming in. Later, around 2 am, I was awoken by some dogs barking. It was normal for them to bark now and then, but had never woken me up before. Something had them really upset, and their barking seemed really frantic.

I got up and went to the front door to see what was going on. I opened the door to see if I could figure out what the problem was. There was a slight breeze coming from the south when all the sudden I was hit in the face with a horrible smell. It was like a combination of wet dog and garbage. It was like nothing I've smelled before. I stood there quietly listening and wondering what the smell was when my eye caught some movement across the street. On the south side of the house across the street, a mysterious figure came walking out. It was darker on that side of the street, but I could tell it had a towering frame. It was able to step over the 4-foot fence like it was nothing. It headed to the road and then stopped. I noticed the dogs had stopped barking and I thought that was very strange. The figure turned and started walking up the road heading from my left to right.

As it got closer, my porch light showed me more detail. It was a large, hairy creature. It had a cone-shaped head and not much neck at all. Its arms hung down almost to its knees, and it walked with a long confident stride. As it got closer, I just stood there frozen on my porch. While it walked by my home, it passed by my truck that was parked on the grass. Still trying to figure out just how big the creature was, I could see that its hip was almost even with my truck door handle. That's when I realized this monster had to be at least 8 and a half feet tall.

As it walked past my driveway, it was only about 30 feet from me, I could see enormous muscles under its dark matted fur. I held my breath and prayed it would keep going and not notice me. It continued walking down the road. I saw it step over the old barbwire fence, and just like that, it was gone. The dogs gave a few more barks, and then the night was silent.

I walked back into the house and got dressed. I thought about walking down the road to look for it. But then I thought about how massive this monster was. I didn't really want to run into this monster in the dark.

I've seen my share of unusual things, but this definitely takes the cake. It's been many years, but I still remember that smell and the sight of that creature as it walked by my home. Its movements were so agile, but it had such a significant presence. I haven't told many people about my sighting, I'm not sure many would believe me. But, it's something I'll never forget.

Uinta Watchers

From James

I spend a lot of time in the outdoors and always have. As I've gotten older, it gets to be less frequent, but in my 20's I spent a lot of time hiking and camping. Most of my adventures were in the Uinta Mountains close to where I grew up central Utah.

The Uinta Mountains have a vibrant history going back to the Native

Americans. The Conquistadors in the 16th and 17th centuries mined for gold in the Uinta until they were driven out by the Native Americans near the beginning of the 18th century. I grew up hearing rumors of people who had come across old Spanish mines, never to be seen again.

The Uinta are also known for their rich paranormal and Sasquatch lore, not to mention UFO and Skinwalkers stories that many people tell. I've heard them all. But honestly, I have only experienced one very frightening incident of my own. It happened in the late '80s near Jordan Lake, its located on the Naturalist Basin hiking trail.

I left where I lived in Salt Lake early on a Wednesday morning. I planned to arrive and head up the trail before noon. That would get me to where I wanted to camp around 2 or 3 o'clock so I could set up camp before dark. It was a beautiful July day, and there wasn't expected to be any significant weather for the week. I was excited to get out of civilization and be by myself for a while.

Everything had gone as planned, and I set up camp just past Jordan Lake. Once everything was set up, I just fished and enjoyed the solitude of nature.

My first day out was uneventful, and I ate dinner then watched the fire before going to bed. That night I fell into a heavy sleep, then I woke in the middle of the night. I'd had a disturbing dream that I was at camp and someone was yelling at me to leave! I had the distinct feeling I wasn't wanted there. It was an alarming and vivid dream that stayed with me all through the night. I slept after the dream, but restlessly. At 5 am, just as it was starting to break light, I decided to get up and make my breakfast. The feeling of the dream was still lingering with me.

After breakfast, I made a day pack and headed out for a long hike. I walked the trail all day, stopping occasionally to fish and watch wildlife. I headed back towards my camp around late afternoon. After I'd gone a reasonable distance back towards camp, I stopped to take a breather. Just then I noticed some movement in the trees to my right. I scanned the trees to get a better look. I was confident I'd see a deer or elk but couldn't find anything. I started back down the trail keeping my eyes on the tree line about 100 yards from me. Every so often, I would see shadows jump from one tree (or bush) to another. I had a horrible feeling that I was being watched. After hiking for another hour, I just knew I was being followed by three or four people in the trees. They were stealthy, probably because they didn't want to be seen. But I was not happy about being all alone in the woods with a group of people following me.

I never traveled in the mountains unarmed, and I had my sidearm with me at all times. It was an old Colt 1911 I had inherited from my grandad. I didn't know whether they were armed or what they might want from me. I pretended to take a break behind a large rock, and I slipped into the tree line. I quickly and quietly worked my way up and behind where I last saw them in the trees. As I got to the spot where they had been, I found nothing. I scanned the area but couldn't see anything.

Confused, I walked down through the area where I was certain I had seen the shadows slipping through the trees. I couldn't find any sign of them there either, I couldn't even find any tracks. I had spent most of my life hunting and hiking, I was an excellent tracker, and I was baffled. I couldn't find any signs that anyone had been in the area.

I walked back to my pack by the rock where I had left it and headed back to camp. I watched closely as I got closer to camp. I hadn't seen anything else, so I thought whatever it was had decided to leave me alone. However, I still couldn't shake the feeling of being watched. I made a fire and cooked dinner. As night began to fall over the mountains, the sense of creepiness got darker and darker.

I started hearing footsteps all around my camp. This continued until I couldn't stand it. I yelled out, "Who's there?! I can hear you!!". It went quiet, and I went back to my fire. I was confused because I knew something was there, and yet nothing was there. Every time I heard something or saw something flash through the trees, it wasn't real.

Every time I checked, I found nothing. As I sat by the fire, all my senses were on edge. I blocked the firelight from my eyes (firelight kills your night vision), so I could try and see what was going on around me. After what felt like an hour or so I started to hear sounds. It sounded like people were talking among the trees. I strained to listen to what they were saying, but it was in a language I couldn't understand. However, I was reasonably sure it was a Native American language.

Suddenly there in between two large trees directly in front of me, there was a dark shadow. I wasn't sure if it had stepped out from behind the tree or materialized there. But it was very tall and had a distinct outline that looked like a Native American warrior. I just stared at it in complete shock. After what felt like forever, it seemed to take a step towards me. I reached down a grabbed my flashlight and shined it towards the figure. As my light got to the spot where the figure was, it vanished. I scanned the area with the flashlight, trying to figure out where it had gone, but whatever it was it had disappeared in the beam of light.

I was scared to death, knowing I was many miles from my vehicle or from anyone else. There was no way I wanted to fumble through the wilderness in the dark to try and leave; I didn't know what to do. I heard the voices start up again but this time seemed to be a chanting which unnerved me even more... I didn't think at this point it was possible to be more frightened. Finally, I decided the best course of action would be to build a big bonfire and keep it going through the night. I gathered as much wood as I could without leaving the light of my campfire. I had gathered enough wood for a week, but I just started burning it all.

I sat with my back to the massive fire all night, feeding it whenever it would start to die. Throughout the night, my panic came in waves. I would just start feeling a little better when the footsteps or chanting would start up again. Each time I built up the fire and yelled out into the night. This went on all night long.

By sun-up, I was exhausted. Both from the adrenaline and lack of sleep.

But there was no way I was spending one more night there. I packed everything up and hiked out, continuously watching my back and the tree line. It is hard to say if I saw anything on my way out because I was so exhausted, I couldn't focus.

I made it to my vehicle and headed for home. I was so grateful to have made it through the night.

As I've looked over my experience, I believe I had somehow camped in a forbidden place. There was a furious spirit there. I've camped many times after this; it never stopped me from camping or enjoying the outdoors. But, I am always a tad bit fearful I may run into another angry spirit of the forest.

Witch Hecida

From Dan

Authors Notes: Growing up in Cache Valley, you hear a lot of stories about Witch Hecida who lives up in Logan Canyon. As I've studied it more, I've run into a lot more urban legends about Witch Hecida and the Nunnery than I have actual first-person stories. When it comes to the Nunnery and Logan Canyon, it's always a story that happened to a friend of a friend or an uncle or aunt. I've always strived to use only first-person accounts in my books. This story is a rare, first-person account, from a man who ran into the notorious Witch Hecida.

To give you some of the backstories of the Nunnery and Witch Hecida, I'll briefly summarize some stories you would hear if you'd grown up living in Cache Valley...

Witch Hecida was once a young student from USU who was taken to a kegger up Logan canyon. She was attacked at the party by some unruly college men, and she drowned in the Logan River. From that day on she haunted the woods, chasing off disorderly young people partying in the area. There are some inconsistencies in the stories of how she shows herself.

Some say she comes in with an eerie mist, others say she shows up like a ball of light or giant orb, sometimes she is said to be a dark figure in the forest. One thing that most the legends have in common is that she is often seen surrounded by a pack of large wild dogs with red eyes. She and her dogs are known to chase people out of the canyon.

The nunnery is sometimes attached to the stories of Witch Hecida. It was built initially as Saint Anne's Retreat. It was a Catholic Retreat about 5 miles up Logan Canyon. There are many stories surrounding Saint Anne's and its demise.

Some believe they have seen the ghost of a former Nun who drowned in the pool. Rumor has it that you can still hear her weeping.

Others believe that there was a hermit that lived somewhere near the Nunnery. As this story goes, he would harass the nuns at the retreat. The story ends with him breaking into Saint Anne's and murdering all the nuns.

None of these stories can be verified...but as with most urban legends, the stories have been told over and over, and things morph and change until the truth is hard to identify. The ever changing stories of Saint Anne's and Witch Hecida have always fascinated me. I have searched for a long time, trying to find a first-hand account of Witch Hecida. When I found and interviewed Dan, I was skeptical at first. However, as we continued our conversation, it became apparent he had had a truly horrifying experience.

Dan's story:

I grew up in Logan in the mid-'80s. My experience happened when I was a Junior in Highschool. Three buddies and I were hanging out during spring break, and we were getting bored. We spent the early evening watching some scary movies at one of my friend's house. At one point someone suggested that we should go up to Logan Canyon and tell ghost stories. We put some firewood in the back of my truck and headed up the canyon. We parked on the bridge above the 3rd Dam and carried the wood back into Spring Hollow. We set up some camp chairs and got the fire going.

After a few hours of hanging out and telling stories, we started to hear some strange things in the woods coming from the canyon to our south. We could hear dogs barking, and what sounded like people walking in the woods.

Being teenage boys, none of us wanted to admit we were afraid. I told my friends I was going to walk around and see if I could find out what was going on. In truth, I needed to use the bathroom, and I didn't want any of them following behind to scare me.

I walked up the trail about 50 yards. I had just found a spot out of sight when I heard something walking down the path in my direction. It sounded like some animals walking. I quickly finished up my business and stepped back onto the trail. It was a clear night, and the moon was out, but under the trees, it was very dark. The sound of the animals had stopped.

I was just about to turn and walk back towards the fire when a light caught my eye. It was a bright orange ball of light about the size of a softball, and it seemed to be floating through the trees. Even though it wasn't hard to see, I couldn't believe my eyes. I felt like my feet were stuck to the ground; I couldn't move. I was mesmerized as it slowly made its way down the trail towards me.

As it came around the last little bend and cleared a big tree about 30 yards from me, it was no longer just a ball of light. A person in a cloak stood next to the tree. It wasn't big, in fact, I'd guess it was no more than 5 feet tall, but its presence was ominous. The dark cloaked figure was illuminated by the orb of light. Now that it was closer, I could clearly see that it was a woman, holding the orb in her right hand at about shoulder height. It looked almost as though she was holding a fireball.

I was just about to say something when there was movement from behind her. Two gigantic dogs walked up on either side of the witch. The dogs looked like wolves with red eyes. Their teeth were bared, and I could physically feel the deep rumble of their growls. I turned and bolted.

I screamed out to my friends, "RUN!!!" as I blurred past the fire and headed for the truck. The terror in my voice must have been enough for my friends because they were right behind me at a dead run. I vaulted over the gate and sprinted to my truck. I was in and trying to get the keys out of my pocket when everyone else piled in and slammed their doors.

"What was that!?" one of them yelled.

I had the keys in my hand, but my stress level was rising as I fumbled to find the right key. It also was very dark, making it hard to get the key in the right place. I finally felt the key slide into the ignition. I was just about to turn the key to start the truck when I looked up to see the ball of light slowly making its way down the trail. There was a split second of silence as everyone looked up and saw the same thing I was seeing.

Then, like an explosion, chaos erupted in the truck with everyone yelling, "Go! GO! GOOO!"

I threw the vehicle in reverse and almost lost control as I backed off the bridge. My tires spun and threw rocks as I hurried to turn on to the main road. I sped down the canyon, trying to get control of my emotions. I explained everything I'd seen to my friends. They all told me they had heard me let out a blood-curdling scream, just before they saw me come into sight and yell, "RUN!" They followed me as fast as they could.

We got back into town, and I dropped everyone off. I headed home and stayed up watching TV until dawn. I've heard many stories of Witch Hecida but had never really believed them. From then on, I never spent a night up Logan Canyon. I don't mind going up there during the day, but I'm always out of there before dark.

Diana's Dead Ringer

From Jim

I graduated from a small town in Colorado in 1990. After graduation, I lived in South America for two years as a missionary for my church. I had a lot of friends in high school, but back then it wasn't as easy to keep up when you were away. Now with email, Facebook, and phones, you can stay connected, but back then it was just "snail mail," and it was easy to lose track of friends.

I came back to my little town after my mission and decided to work for the summer before heading off to Utah for school. I got a job installing and repairing PCs. I remember getting called out to do an install at a house, and as I drove into the driveway, the house seemed so familiar. An older lady that I didn't recognize answered the door, but the layout of the house seemed so recognizable to me. As I walked into the front room, it hit me; this was my friend Diana's house. I had been there a few times on double dates. I had several classes with Diana in High School, and we had been on a few dates during my junior and senior year.

After I was done with the installation, I asked the woman of the home how long she had lived there and whether she knew Diana. She explained she and her husband had purchased the house from the family that owned it before. They sold it after their daughter had passed away. I was shocked. I asked if she knew the name of the girl. She said she didn't but knew she was 19 at the time of her death. I thanked her and left.

I couldn't get the thought out of my head, so I went to the library and found Diana's obituary. She died from botched appendicitis surgery. I drove to the cemetery and saw her grave. I felt terrible that I hadn't heard of her passing. It took me a few days to get over the unexpected loss of my friend.

Time passed on, I finished college in Utah, got married, and settled down. One Thanksgiving in the early 2000s, my wife and I traveled back to my home town to visit my family. It was almost dinner time, and my mother asked me if I would run to the store to get some whipped cream. I jumped in the car and headed to the store. It was crowded with shoppers, because of the holiday, and because it was the only store open in town. I made my way to the dairy aisle, trying hard to avoid bumping into the other shoppers. I grabbed the cream and turned to head for the front of the store. I turned the corner into the nearest aisle and ran right into a cart. I apologized, and as I looked up to make eye contact, my mouth hung open with surprise. The woman pushing the cart looked just like my friend Diana. I shook my head, snapped back to my senses, and apologized again for running into her.

She looked at me and asked, "Jim is that you?"

I looked again, still not understanding what was going on. "yea, It's me."

Her face broke into a big smile, "It's Diana, we went to school together."

I smiled and gave her a big hug. But inside, I was very lost. I asked her how she had been. After a minute of small talk, I couldn't hold my question in any longer. "I heard you got sick after high school."

She said, "Ya, I had terrible appendicitis. I almost died, but I pulled through."

We continued catching up for a few minutes, and then I left. I was so confused.

I put the cream on a random shelf in the aisle and left without getting it. I immediately drove five miles to the cemetery. I remembered coming here years back and looking at her grave. When I got to the spot where her gravesite was, it was someone else's headstone. I dove up and down the cemetery, but I couldn't find it her grave. I drove home in a complete stupor. I knew I hadn't dreamed it. I remembered it vividly. I was sad for days when I'd seen her name on that gravestone years ago, I had read her obituary.

I had lived a life where Diana had died, and yet that day I found that she is very much alive. After getting back to my parents, I sat down with my wife and told her the story. She couldn't explain it either. She remembered me telling her about my good friend Diana who had passed away so young.

Today, I am friends with Diana on Facebook. I'm glad to have my friend back, but I've never been able to explain how time changed for me.

Lights

From Tiffany

I grew up loving the paranormal. Ghost stories, campfire stories, you name it, I loved it! But I'd never had an experience of my own until one July night camping. I grew up in Idaho, with the wilderness at my back door. It was a tradition in my family to camp, and we did it all the time.

I was 19 and had just graduated from high school. My family left on a

Tuesday to set up camp at Island Park which is west of Yellowstone. I couldn't get off work till late Wednesday. So, I had packed up early Thursday in my car and headed to Island Park to meet up with my family. I got there around noon, and we had lunch.

After lunch, we floated the river and then hiked a bit. It seemed like there should have been more people there in July. I just passed it off with the thought that there were probably more people spending time in Yellowstone Park rather than here on the outskirts.

We enjoyed our day and ate dinner. I took a cat nap and then got up to enjoy the campfire. It was my younger brother, younger sister, and my Mom and Dad at camp. It was getting late when my bother announced he was headed off to "water the plants." Mom frowned, and I gently threw a rock at his feet as he made his way off into the trees.

We were laughing and having a good time when my brother came running back to camp. "You have to see this!" He exclaimed between deep breaths. We jumped up and asked what it was, but he just motioned for us to follow him and headed back into the trees. We all got up to go see what it was he was looking at. Just as we made it through the trees, I could see bright white lights shining in front of us. We walked about 75 more yards, and there was a clearing in the trees. What we saw was definitely a strange sight. All around, there were bright white balls of light hanging in mid-air. They were so bright; it was hard to look directly at them. They varied in size. Some were the size of a tennis ball and there a few as large as a basketball. We gasped in awe as we walked into the clearing. There was no sound coming from the orbs, but you could feel an electrical surge in the air.

I counted 15 different lights in an area about the size of half a football field. We watched in amazement when my brother announced: "I'm going to touch one."

My dad grabbed him before he could and wouldn't let him get any closer. "What are they?" I asked, but no one said a word. Suddenly one at a time they closed up almost like an eye closing and poof they were gone. We stood there in awe. We waited a while to see if they would come back, but they didn't. We walked back to camp, talking about what we had witnessed, but no one had any good ideas as to what we had just seen.

We watched the next night, but the lights never returned. I've camped in that area many times since, but the lights have never returned. It's strange to think about what it was we saw that night. I'll never forget those lights.

Sasquatch in the Windrivers

From Jon

It was a beautiful July week to hike the Windrivers. It's a wildlife range on the Western side of Wyoming that runs 160 miles from Jackson Hole, south towards South Pass. I have always loved hiking and camping in that area.

I took four days off to hike and fish. I'd planned a 25-mile hike in and 25 miles out. One of the things I like most about the Windrivers is the fact that you could go days without seeing another person. I saw a few hikers coming out on my first day, the rest of my trip, I was all alone in the wilderness.

The first three days went without a hitch. I hiked, fished, read my book, and enjoyed my time in the great outdoors. The only part of my trip that had me bothered was the last day before I walked out. I had an eerie feeling I wasn't alone. It was just this sense, at the back of my mind that kept pricking at me now and then. I chalked it up to having been alone for three days. I let it go and prepared my meal for the evening. I cooked dinner, watched the fire for a while, and then crawled into bed for excellent night sleep.

I woke around 2 am to a loud thump. I sat up in my sleeping bag with my hairs prickling down my neck. My biggest fear was that it might be a bear. This was a big area for bears, and they have a tendency to not be afraid of people. I followed all the normal precautions. I hung my food in a tree and didn't keep food in my tent. But, I'm sure after three days of hiking I smelled pretty badly myself. I could hear the padding of footsteps, and I sat listening intently for the normal grunting that confirm that there was a bear in camp, but I couldn't hear anything.

That's when I realized that it was actually a lot quieter than it should be.

I sat awake listening for what felt like an eternity when I heard the heavy footsteps again. I realized it couldn't be the footsteps of an animal, it seemed like something big walking on two feet. It was coming down out of the trees to my left. There was a hill that direction, to the south of where I was camping. My heart was pounding in my chest as the steps came closer to my camp. It started a fair distance away, and in a brief amount of time was standing in the middle of my camp.

The creature sounded like it was about 5 feet from my tent. I was horrified as I heard it breathing deeply. It was the breathing of an enormous beast, and it was only feet from my bed. At this point, my mind was trying to make a list of all the different things that could be standing on two feet in my camp. I could hear it take a few steps towards my fire that was long since dead. I listened as the creature rummaged through my pack and walked around the fire. I was trying hard not to breathe too loud, but I was sure the creature could hear my heart pounding in my chest. Suddenly the beast took a step towards my tent; I could see a broad dark outline of the creature cover my tent. The moon was full, so I could clearly see the massive silhouette. I could make out a hairy shoulder and arm shadow outlined on my tent.

I was frozen with fear! I knew that what was outside my tent was a Sasquatch. I'd heard many stories but never thought I would be this close to the beast himself. Suddenly, I saw a giant hand reach out, and I saw the hand actually touch my tent. The hand lightly pushed the side of the tent, as though it was testing the surface or feeling the fabric. The size of the hand was so large, and the creature was so immense, I expected it to grab the tent and rip it up off the ground with me still in it. Just as I was about to scream out, it stopped rubbing the tent and removed its hand. After another moment or two, it turned and took off walking down the path. I listened as the heavy footsteps moved farther and farther away.

I couldn't sleep. I sat quietly listening all night, but the creature never returned. After it was light enough, I climbed out of my tent and found I could hardly stand up. Every muscle in my body hurt. It took a moment to realize it was because I had spent hours with every muscle in my body tensed. I stretched and walked around. I found enormous footprints coming down the hill and walking around my camp, which just confirmed what I believed had happened. I had been visited by a Sasquatch. I ate my breakfast and packed up for the hike out. I'd gone from extreme fear in the middle of the night, to more of excitement this morning. I hiked out, thinking about what had happened. By the time I reached my car, I'd come to the conclusion that I felt blessed to have had an encounter with the elusive King of Cryptids.

Small Gods and Missing Signatures

From Jarrett

I have always loved books. Ever since Highschool, I've loved the work of Terry Pratchett. He writes comedic fantasy, and most of his books are centered around what he called the disc world. I had read all of his books and was always one of the first people at the book store to buy his new one as soon as they came out. My very favorite book was called "Small Gods." I probably read it 20 times by the time I was 20 years old.

I was born and raised in Washington state. So the thought of meeting Terry, who lived in England was very remote at best. One day as I was browsing through eBay, I found a first edition signed copy of *Small Gods*! I quickly figured the maximum I could pay, and in the last few minutes of the auction, I posted my bid. To my amazement, I won. The book became the prized center of my book collection. I build a bookshelf in my front room to display my favorite books with *Small Gods* as the jewel and centerpiece. When my wife and I sold the house, and we began construction on our new home, I package up my book collection and put it in storage.

After a year of construction, I was able to build a new book self in my "Man Cave". I was excited to get my books out of storage. I found them all, safely stored in the duct-taped Rubbermaid storage containers where I'd left them. I started unpacking and organizing my books. I found my copy of *Small Gods.* It was carefully bubble wrapped, in its own small box. It was taped up just as I'd left it. I opened it up, excited to see it again. I opened it and turned to the title page, but something was missing...... the signature of Terry Pratchett was gone! I flipped through my first edition book, but there was no signature to be found.

I was dumbfounded. I unpacked my other books to make sure they were all accounted for. Everything was there. The only thing missing was the Author's signature. I began to flip through other first additions I had and other books with author signatures. The signatures were still in those books. Still confused, I started to look through my other Terry Pratchett books. As I did, I found my first edition book *Night Watch* was now signed!

To this day I don't know what happened, I wasn't confused, I wasn't mistaken. I remember when I put the books in storage, it was my *Small Gods* that was signed not *Night watch*. It's not so valuable that someone would have stolen it to replace it with an unsigned first addition.

I believe I must have gone through some type of shift in reality. Something altered my history but why, and how...I may never know.

The Book

From Tara

For a long time, I was a book broker and collector. I guess I'm still a collector, but I don't hunt books for people anymore. Once the internet became so accessible, no one really needed a book broker anymore. It was the early 80's when I had my experience with the Paranormal. I was living in Bend, Oregon.

I always wondered if the older books I found held anything unusual in them. Books are a strange thing, people become very attached to them. Both collectors and everyday people can have unique connections to a book. I've had a few books over time that I felt had a strange aura around them. I never told anyone about it because I thought they might think I was crazy. To be 100% honest, I wasn't sure it was even possible. That is until I got *The Beasts of Tarzan* book.

I purchased the Tarzan book from an estate sale. I would often go to estate sales and browse through the books, looking for a gem here or there. Not many people are aware of the rarity of some books. I always had a list of what was looking out for. This book wasn't on anyone radar at the time. Tarzan books aren't super rare, but this one was in excellent condition, it wasn't a first edition which would have been amazing, but it was an older copy. They were only asking a couple of bucks for it, so I figured if I couldn't sell it, I wouldn't mind having it for my own collection. It had a beautiful light green cover, and as I looked through it, I found a name and date written in pencil in the back "Benjamin 1920". I paid for the book and left for home.

When I got home, I put the book on my desk and forgot about it. The very next morning, I got up and headed to the kitchen to get some breakfast. When I passed my office, I noticed that the book was on the floor. In fact, it looked like it had been placed on the floor. It was open as if someone had been reading it. I found this very odd. I lived alone except for my dog D'Artagnan, and he had been with me all night. I picked the book up and looked at it. I was afraid that if it had fallen off my desk, it would have damaged the spine, as old as it was. I breathed a sigh of relief when I realized it was fine. I shook it off and figured I had accidentally bumped it off my desk when I'd walked away the night before.

Over the next few weeks, I found the book four more times on the floor. It was always open in the same spot on the floor and was always turned to the same pages. After the fourth time, I decided to put the book in my old trunk. It was in the corner of my office, and it was where I kept some of my more valuable books under lock and key.

It was quiet for a few days, and so I forgot all about the book. Then all hell broke loose. I was reading a book before going to bed when D'Artagnan jumped up as if he heard a noise. His hackles stood up on end, and he started to growl at the hallway. At first, I couldn't hear anything then I heard it... It was a deep thudding. I got out of bed and told D'Artagnan to quiet down. He sat on the end of the bed, still staring down the hall. I walked down the hall and could hear that the thumping was coming from the office. I opened the door and realized that the hollow thud was the sound of someone pounding on my old trunk in the corner of the room.

I reached into the room and flipped on the light to get a better look, and suddenly, the sound stopped! I walked over to the trunk, but couldn't see any signs of anyone having been there. I got the key from my desk drawer and opened it, half expecting an animal to jump out. As I opened the lid, I found nothing out of the ordinary. I closed the lid and looked around. I was stumped as to what could have caused the banging.

I checked all the doors and windows and went back to bed. I had just gotten back into bed when I heard the banging start up again. I ran down the hall with D'Atagnan on my heels, and as I opened the office door again, it stopped.

My nerves were good and frayed by now. I left the light on in the office and went back to bed. The sound didn't come back that night, but my mind was running wild, trying to figure out what was going on.

Things were quiet for about a week. Then one night, I was startled out of a deep sleep when the door to my bedroom was flung open, and my dog started barking at the hallway. I jumped out of bed and grabbed the phone, thinking I had an intruder. I was just about to dial 911 when I heard the distinctly familiar sound of the trunk being hammered on. I knew with certainty then; it was not an intruder. I walked down the hall, and just as before, turned on the light to the office, and the banging stopped. I was both terrified and stumped. I was starting to wonder what I had brought into my house to cause this.

It went another week without any sound from my new ghost friend. I was just beginning to believe it may have left me alone for good. I was very wrong...

I had gone to bed and fallen into a deep sleep. I remember rolling over in bed when the smell of burning wood permeated my nose. I was trying to figure out if I was awake or dreaming when a new horrible burnt smell hit me.

I sat up in bed and instinctively reached to turn on my lamp. Just before turning it on I froze with a gasp. Standing right next to my bed was a boy of about 10 years old, he had clothes on from another era, including a gray newsboy hat. The left side of his body was burned black. I could see one of his eyes was burned out, and there were tendrils of smoke drifting up from his smoldering clothes. I could see a few red cinders still burning in his shirt. I recognized the horrible burning smell now as burning hair and flesh. I was horrified and unable to move. He looked at me with an angry, almost accusing look. He started to speak, but I couldn't hear what he was saying. He looked at me again, and with a considerable effort, he spoke aloud this time.

I could hear him in a soft raspy voice. "You took my book." He leaned in closet to me and again spoke, "You took my book."

It hit me like a ton of bricks, I was looking at Benjamin, the owner of the Tarzan book. Then with a flash of dark smoke, he evaporated. The next thing I remember was waking in the morning. I was still so terrified, but I couldn't understand whether what I saw was real or a nightmare? I got up and retrieved the book. I sat in the kitchen, shaken from my experience. I didn't know what to do. However, I knew without a doubt that this book wasn't going to spend one more night in my house.

It happened to be a Sunday morning, so I dressed and went for a drive. I felt that if I destroyed the book, Benjamin might stay at my home, and I didn't want that. I called Jim, a friend of mine, who was also a book broker. I met Jim that afternoon and explained what I had experienced. At first, I thought he would think I was crazy, but he listened intently.

He explained that he had also had a similar experience once. He told me he found a gentleman who collected books just like this one. He explained he thought this guy would love to have the Tarzan book. Jim offered to take the book to him and split any money he got on the sale. I told him if he took the book, he was welcome to the entire sale. I handed off the book and went back home.

I'm happy to say I never experienced another incident attached to that book. I don't know what had happened to Benjamin, how he died or why he was so attached to the book. Not long after this incident, I started renting a storage unit for all my older books. I have Benjamin to thank for that.

Old Neighbors

By Ed

My wife and I had been married for about 3 years, and I had just finished school. We bought a home in an older town in Northern Utah. It was the perfect home for us with plenty of room to grow. I just found a job and was looking forward to working at a new company. It was about 30 miles South, so the commute wasn't going to be a problem. My wife was planning on finding a job after we settled in, and we were excited to get our life started.

The home was the perfect fixer-upper, and I'd worked remodeling homes for years. I knew I could do everything that was needed to make it look perfect. Our house was in an older part of town, there was a fenced-in a meadow on one side of us and an old house next door. The house next door was in bad shape. It was old, the windows were dusty, the lawn was trimmed but dead, and there were weeds in the driveway cracks. We weren't sure if anyone actually lived there or not. The realtor wasn't sure when I asked her, but I figured we'd eventually find out. As we were moving boxes into the house, I would sometimes glance next door. A couple times, the curtains in the upstairs window moved as if someone was maybe looking out at us but stepping away quickly when we turned to look. I shrugged it off and kept moving things in.

After moving in and getting settled, I walked over to the house next door and knocked on the front door. No one answered, so I left. As time went on, we fell into a routine. I often worked in the yard, and we would both come and go from work and other activities. Still, I was always a little curious about the house next door.

I could swear, now and then, that I'd catch a glimpse of someone in the upstairs window looking out at me. A few times I saw the curtains move to the side like a hand was pulling the curtains back, but I couldn't be sure. Now and then, I'd go over and knock on the door. No one ever answered, and we never saw anyone come or go from the house.

One afternoon I was raking up leaves in the back yard when some movement caught my eye. Between our yard and the yard next door, there was a wooden fence. You had to be close to the wall to see anything between the wooden slats, but there was about half an inch gap between the bottom of the fence and the grass. I could see the outline of shoes walking back and forth along the wall. As I looked closer, I could just make out the general shape of someone walking from the back of their yard to the front.

I walked over towards the fence and called out a hello. I was met with silence. Confused, I called out hello again, this time a little louder, but still heard nothing. I walked over to the shed, grabbed a five-gallon bucket, and walked over to the fence. I put the bucket down and stood on it so I could see over the wall. The fence was about six and a half feet tall. I stood up and looked over to find absolutely nothing. The grass was still trimmed but dead with weeds growing here and there. It looked abandoned, but I knew I had seen someone walking along the fence line. I had seen their outline and their shoes. Puzzled, I went back to my raking.

That night, I asked my wife what she thought, but she said she hadn't noticed anything peculiar about the house other than the fact that it was old and looked abandoned. I started to wonder if someone was squatting there that didn't want to be found. But I wasn't sure.

One morning I woke up and got ready for work. I was just about to head out the door when my wife reminded me it was trash day, and I needed to take the can to the road. I cursed under my breath because it was raining really hard. I had forgotten to do it the night before. I threw on my coat and went out the side door. I grabbed the garbage can and headed for the street. I turned the can towards the road and turned back towards my car when I froze. There on the porch of the house, next door was an old lady in a dress sitting in a rocking chair. Next to her, leaning on the porch's support post was an old man. He was mostly bald and had overalls on. He was smoking a pipe, and they were staring at me. They both looked angry as they just stared at me from their front porch. I waved and thought about going over, but I was getting soaked and needed to head to work. I looked back at them as I ran back to the house, and they just continued to glare wordlessly at me. I quickly told my wife about what I saw, then I got in my car to head for work. As pulled out of the driveway, I looked one last time, and the couple was gone from the porch. I shrugged and thought about how strange that was.

A few days later a truck pulled up to the house next door, and an older gentleman got out and went in the front door. I figured this was my chance to find out what was going on. I walked over to the front porch, as I was about to knock the man came out. I introduced myself and asked if he lived in the house. He introduced himself as Todd and explained it was his house, but no one lived there.

He said it had been his parent's house, and the house he grew up in. He told me he tried to keep it maintained, but after his parents died, he didn't have the heart to sell it. I felt a little shocked at the news that it was empty. I told him what I had seen in the rain and what I'd experienced since moving in. He gave a little laugh and said, "Yep, that's my Mom and Dad, they never really liked people they didn't know. I'm sure they don't mean you any harm."

I thanked him and walked home. Over the next four years, I had a few experiences with the ghosts next door. Eventually, Todd sold the land. A new family demolished and built their home where the old house used to be. I never asked if the new neighbors had any problems, but I assumed the ghosts left when the house did. The old house was very creepy but never evil. It was a very a strange experience living next to spirits.

Enchanted Choir

From Eddy

I'm a member of the Church of Jesus Christ of Latter-Day Saints, and in my church, we often have jobs that we are asked to do. Everything is voluntary and so depending on what your calling is, you could do all kinds of things. In the early 2000s, part of my calling was to lock up the church building every night. It might seem like an easy job, but if you've ever tried to kick out a group of young men playing basketball at 10 pm when the game tied, you might agree that it's not always a piece of cake.

This church building was an older one. There were a lot of areas inside to check when it was time to lock up. Most nights were typical, check and lock all the doors. Make sure the windows are closed, and the lights are off. Kick out anyone after 10:00 pm.

I was never afraid to lock up, what could be scary about a church? Not to mention, I was a 30-year-old adult man, I could take care of myself. I never imagined that I would run into anything paranormal at the church; I was dead wrong.

It was a Wednesday night, and I showed up at 9:45 to lock up. I walked in and started checking rooms. I had checked each one of the classrooms, and as I got closer to the chapel, I heard music. It's not entirely uncommon for people to come and practice playing the piano or the organ for their own Sunday calling. I walked down to the doors of the chapel, and I realized it wasn't just the organ, I could hear a choir singing. I huffed under my breath because I absolutely hated kicking people out of the church, especially a group of people.

I looked at my watch and realized it was just 9:50, so I figured I'd check that everything else was locked up then ask them to leave. The parking lot had been empty when I pulled in, but it wasn't-unusual for people to walk to the church as it was in the middle of the small town. I walked around checking classrooms and bathrooms, making sure everything was locked up and all the windows were shut. Kids had been known to leave a window unlocked so they could sneak in to play basketball. As I walked the hallway, I kept thinking about how beautiful the choir sounded even out here in the hall. I thought at least I had some beautiful music to listen to while I locked up.

Finally, I had everything locked up, and it was now 10:15. I had hoped the choir would have stopped on their own, but they hadn't. I walked down to the door near the front of the chapel. The choir was singing "How Great Thou Art." I decided I would wait until they finished the song then let them know it was time to go. As I stood outside the door, the song sounded beautiful. I stood patiently and waited. Just as the song finished, I opened the door and walked in. I was met with a dark room and complete silence. I was baffled. I walked over and flipped on the lights next to the first pew. The chapel lit up, and to my shock, it was empty.

I walked in and said, "Hello!?" I expected a bunch of people to jump up and say BOO but again I was hit with nothing but silence. I walked up to the area where the choir would be and then passed the organ and nothing were there. I looked at the organ. The organ I had heard perfectly accompany a beautiful choir a few moments earlier, was turned off. I should have been frightened, but I wasn't. Somehow I felt I had been a witness to something amazing that I couldn't understand. I turned off the lights and walked out. I locked the last door and stood in the cold night for a moment and breathed it in. I felt blessed to have been a part of something fascinating. I continued to lock up each night for the rest of the year, then the job was passed on to someone else. I never heard the choir again, but every time I walked in, I secretly hoped I would.

I Just Missed, Myself

From Tiffani

It was a beautiful spring day in May of 2003, and I was a senior in High School. I'd spent the entire day talking with my friends, finishing up my classes and overall just enjoying the time. I was excited to be going to college in the fall, and life was amazing. I never thought I would randomly have a run-in with the unknown.

I finished up school for the day and said goodbye to my friends Trina and Kim. We had planned on meeting up around 7 pm to hang out at Kim's. I knew I had to get home, check-in, do some laundry, and have dinner with my parents before then. I was the youngest of four and the last kid at home, so my mother had made sure I was always home for dinner. I think she was hanging on so she didn't have to feel like an empty nester yet.

I drove out of the school parking lot and headed home. I looked at my hand and saw the star I had drawn on the back of my hand this morning. I cursed as I realized it was a reminder to drop off my library book, *Foundation's Triumph* by David Brin. It was now a month past due, I couldn't ever seem to remember to return it. I turned right at the next corner and headed for the library. There was a parking spot right up front so I parked and went to the door. Just before I opened it, I realized I didn't have the $2 to pay the late fee, so I slipped the book in the return slot and told myself I would pay it next time I went in. I have always been an avid reader, from the time I was little, and even as a teenager; I went through books reasonably fast.

I jumped back into my car and headed home. I pulled into the driveway, gathered my things from the back seat, and walked into the kitchen. My mother was sitting at the table looking over her cookbook, and she looked up at me with a shock on her face. "How did you do that?" she asked.

I looked at her with a shrug and asked: "What are you talking about?".

She looked at me and said, "How did you get back outside? I didn't see you leave."

Now I was confused. "What are you talking about? I just got home from school." I explained.

She looked frightened and asked again how I did it.

I said, "I told you, I just got home."

Just at that moment, there was a bang from my room that was upstairs, just above where we were talking. My mother looked concerned. I looked at my mother, and she explained that I had come home about 10 minutes ago. I had told her about my day and then went up to my room. I thought she was kidding, but I could see in her face she was very serious.

She asked if I was playing a joke on her, and I reassured her that I was not. There was really no way to get from my room outside without my mother seeing me leave. We walked upstairs together and turned towards my bedroom door. It was shut, and we couldn't hear anything inside. I opened the door and found nothing. There was no one inside my room. I looked through my closet and under my bed but couldn't find anything out of the ordinary. My mother checked my window, and it was locked from the inside.

We sat on the bed, and my mother was shaking. She recounted what had happened in the last 20 minutes or so. She told me I had walked in and said "hi." She had asked how my day was, and I said it was great. I had apparently told her I was going to do some laundry so I could go after dinner to hang out at Kim's. Then I had run upstairs. Immediately after I'd run up the stairs, she hears the door bang behind her. That's when she turned around and saw the 'other me' walk into the house. We both sat there, dumbfounded. What had my mother experienced?

After a few minutes of trying to figure it all out, my mother walked back downstairs to figure out what she was going to cook for dinner. I sat for a few minutes trying to understand what had happened. If my mother wasn't so upset, I might have thought she was playing a trick on me. I stood up to start gathering my laundry when something caught my eye.

Sitting right there on my desk was my book. The book I had just dropped off at the library less than 20 minutes ago. I walked over and picked it up. There it was, in my hand, *Foundation's Triumph*! I flipped through the book and looked at the front. It had the old card in it and my name and date I had checked it out. Now I was utterly baffled. I knew I'd dropped it off; I had looked at the cover right before putting it in the slot at the library. I walked downstairs and showed my mom.

I explained what I had done and how I had dropped this very book off, but now it was back at my desk. I told her how I had put it in my bag this morning and put the star on my hand to remind me to drop it off. My mother grabbed her jacket, and we both went out to the car. We drove down to the library, talking back and forth about what could have happened. What did it all mean? We got to the Library, and we walked in, and my Mom made up a story. She explained to the librarian that I had left some notes inside a book I dropped off asked if she could check the return bin for the book.

The Librarian walked over, opened the box, and pulled out the three books inside, but none of them was my book. I asked if someone had maybe taken it out, but she explained she was the only one working that afternoon and she hadn't checked it until we asked. We thanked her for her help and walked out. My mother and I drove home in silence. When my dad got home, we tried to explain it to him. In the end, he thought we both had just gotten confused. I've never experienced anything like this before or since. My mother and I still talk about it, but neither of us has a clue what it was we experienced that afternoon.

Ghost, Spirit, or Divine Intervention?

From Julie

It was mid-summer of 1971 in the small town of Kearns, Utah and I was 15 years old. I was bored one day and wanted to do something, so I headed down the hill to my best friend's home two miles away. I was told that she was gone shopping and would be home soon, so I strolled around Kearns to pass the time. A Toyota with two teenagers stopped and asked me if I needed a ride. I politely declined, but they continued talking with me. I remember asking them where they were from. Kearns was so small at that time; it was a rarity to see someone you didn't recognize. I'd never seen them around. They said they were from Magna, so I asked if they know my cousins? They didn't, but talked to me for a few minutes and left.

I got tired of walking around and waiting for my friend, so I headed back up the hill towards home. Once again, the Toyota with the two guys drove up and asked me if I needed a ride. They told me they would drop me off at my house before heading home to Magna. After walking around town for quite some time, I was getting tired and was pretty thirsty. Thinking back now, it was a stupid idea...but I accepted a ride with them the rest of the way to my house. I didn't want to walk the rest of the way up the hill.

Once in the tiny vehicle, I was squished between the two massive guys in the front seat. I was wedged pretty tightly between them. As I looked around, I noticed a red rose on the visor of the passenger side. Making conversation, I asked where they got the beautiful red rose from. They told me it was from the funeral of the person they killed. I remember thinking that was a weird thing to say. As we approached my street, I thanked them and asked to get out. They started laughing and drove past my house.

I lived on the last urban street in Kearns at that time. Past my house, the area consisted mostly of dirt fields and a road leading out to a company called Hercules. This area between my house and Hercules was not developed because of all the testing they were doing at that time. There were no homes or stores along that road, it was only really traveled by employees going to and from work. On the weekends it was barely traveled at all.

My fear started to grow as they passed my house and turned left onto a dirt road. I knew the area well because I used to ride my bike there, there was nothing past this point; there was no one around to save me. Now I was terrified! Just then, both boys started pawing at me. Somehow, I was able to wriggle out of the car window and onto the ground. The driver was a pretty heavy guy, so it was nothing short of a miracle that I was able to get out. I was stunned a little from the fall, but I jumped up and started running as fast as I could. I glanced back, and I could see dirt flying from their car as they were turning around to follow me. It was as if I was running faster than humanly possible. I sprinted towards the main road as fast as my legs would carry me.

When I reached the main road, a large RV stopped. They opened their door as if they had been expecting to pick me up at that very spot. I practically dove in, any place was better than where I had been just minutes ago! I was so relieved when I looked up and saw an elderly couple. They smiled at me but didn't say a word as I got in. I thanked them as a hastily explained my situation, all the while trying to catch my breath. My heart was still pounding in my chest. They drove me towards home. The two of them never said a word to me; they just kept smiling at me and quietly comforting me. The RV stopped when I said, "Right here." As I stepped out, I saw the Toyota speeding towards me as I ran across the street. I was so scared and running so hard, that I practically leaped over my chain-linked fence, only needing to stick my foot into one link. In a matter of seconds, I was in my house behind the locked door.

The next day I was at Liberty Park sitting on the grass with my best friend. I was telling her what happened to me when the Toyota drove by us. As they saw me, they speed away with a scared look in their eyes.

As I told my friend the story, I started to realize just how odd it was that an RV would have been traveling on that road at that moment. Even more strange that they were headed the direction that I needed to go. They never said a thing to me. Were they ghosts? Where they angels? Whatever they were, they were definitely part of some sort of divine intervention that saved me that day.

The Paper Route

From Joshua

I grew up in a small town in Nevada. It was the kind of town where everyone knew each other. I was 12 years old when I told my dad I wanted a job. He didn't take me too seriously at first, but over time, I was quite persistent. Finally, once he figured I wasn't going to let it go, he helped me get a job as a paperboy. The paper wasn't really a newspaper, it was more of an advertisement flyer that went out three to four times a week. At first, I was really excited. I would run home from school, fold up the papers, and head out on my afternoon route. Because it was an advertisement paper, the company demanded I hang them on every door in my six-block area. After a week, I got tired of hanging them and started tossing them on the porch. My boss called my Dad first, and then me. He wanted to make sure I knew I needed to *hang* them on every door, or I'd be fired. I wouldn't have cared, but my Dad, who helped me find the job, took this very seriously, so I went back to hanging them.

One house on my route always gave me the creeps. It was an older home, and the old man that lived there would always ran into the house or hide behind the curtains when I came by to hang the paper. I didn't know who he was. This was especially strange because I thought I knew everyone in town. I asked my dad one night what was wrong with him. My Dad explained he was a World War II Veteran. When he got home from the war, he had never been the same. He worked as a janitor, but no one could get him to talk. In fact, no one had heard him speak since before the war.

For the next month I continued to do my paper route, always dreading that old house, until one day when I didn't see the old man. I was perplexed and a bit relieved. I quickly placed the paper and took off. However, the next visit, I wasn't so lucky. I opened the gate to the yard and walked up to the porch. I placed the paper in the handle, and as I turned back towards the gate, some movement caught my eye. There was a tall bush at the corner of the house. Just to the side of it was the old man, peeking from around the hedge at me. I jumped and let out a yell.

As I stared, he looked at me with wide eyes. He seemed to be trying to speak, but nothing was coming out. He looked pale and frightened. My heart caught in my throat, and I ran for my bike. Flying through the gate, I took off as fast as I could. I fumbled with the rest of my papers and took off to deliver the last few of them and then headed home. I told my Dad I wanted to quit and tried to explain how scared I was of the old man. He wasn't having any of it. I went to bed that night dreading my next route in 2 days.

The next delivery day came, and I skipped the old man's house. As I was about to throw the extra paper away, my Dad caught me. After a stern lecture, I mounted my bike and headed to the old house. I looked around didn't see anyone. I ran through the gate and to the porch quickly, I hung the paper and tried to leave…. As I turned, I'm pretty sure all the blood left my face. There between me and the gate was the old man. I had no idea how he got there so fast. His eyes were wide, and he looked pale and had a pained expression on his face. He reached out to me with one hand and was trying to speak, but all that came out was a gurgle….

I took off, running around him. I half expected him to grab me, but I didn't feel anything. I don't remember if I ran through the gate or over it, but I took off like a shot on my bike. I was horrified, I did not want to go back EVER again. I decided that I would do a better job of hiding his paper because I sure wasn't going to deliver it.

Two days later, as I was delivering the paper to the house next to the old man's, I saw three or four cars outside. I drove by slowly to see what was going on. People were going in and out, going through stuff.

After my route, I asked my Dad about it. He drove down to see what was going on, but I refused to go with him. After an hour, he came home and took me in the front room and asked me a few questions.

He asked, "When was the last time I saw the old man?"

I told him it was two days ago. I explained how he had scared me to death during the last two trips to his house. My dad was quiet for a moment. Finally, he told me how the old had died in his home, but he hadn't been found for a while. He had been dead for over a week, alone in his house, before anyone checked on him. I couldn't believe it, I know without a doubt I saw the old man!

I've gone over it in my mind for years. I believe the old man had died and was just trying to get me to go find him. I now believe he wasn't trying to scare me, he just wanted to let me know he was inside. It's an experience I'll never forget.

ABOUT THE AUTHOR

John Olsen lives in Lewiston, Utah in beautiful Cache Valley with his wife and 3 children. He has spent 30+ years researching and collecting paranormal stories for this book series. John is still collecting stories and would love to hear from you. You can contact him at olsenj243@gmail.com

Made in the USA
Middletown, DE
30 August 2020

16893148R00076